Holiness in the Midst of Everyday Life

by
John Wesley

Schmul Publishing Company
Nicholasville, Kentucky

Cover image copyright: <a href='https://www.123rf.com/profile_viewapart'>viewapart / 123RF Stock Photo</a>. Used by permission.

Published by Schmul Publishing Co.
PO Box 776
Nicholasville, KY 40340
USA

Printed in the United States of America

ISBN 10: 0-88019-603-3
ISBN 13: 978-0-88019-603-1

Visit us on the Internet at www.wesleyanbooks.com, or order direct from the publisher by calling 800-772-6657, or by writing to the above address.

Contents

Foreword

IT IS HARD FOR us today to fully appreciate the nature and extent of the opposition Wesley encountered in the early days of the Eighteenth Century Evangelical revival. Although thousands of common people flocked to hear the outdoor preaching of this young and controversial Church of England cleric, many of his fellow Anglican clergy, including his father's own Epworth parish successor, were unwilling to allow him to preach inside the consecrated walls of their churches. Other critics of the revival attacked Methodism in print, or when that proved ineffectual, instigated mob violence against the Wesley brothers and their supporters. Noted for his composure in the face of mobs, John Wesley was no less adept in confronting his more civil, if equally dangerous, theological critics. In defending the evangelical revival and the early preaching of Methodism, Wesley articulated the central tenets of his movement and established a model for sane and serious discussion of controversial, if deeply held, religious beliefs. Although repeatedly falsely caricatured and vilified, Wesley maintained his dignity, refusing to stoop to the tactics of his most vicious critics.

Published in 1742, *The Character of a Methodist* remains one of the most beautifully written and powerful defenses of the Evangelical revival. Wesley's purpose was twofold. First he argued that Methodism was merely authentic Christianity. It did not employ an odd vocabulary, or peculiar dress or food, or unusual marriage customs. Its central teachings were the common property of all evangelical believers.

Secondly, Wesley insisted that the distinguishing mark of a Methodist was merely the undivided love of God and neighbor. As he noted years later, *The Character of a Methodist* was really his first writing on the subject of Christian Perfection. Boldly stating that "a tree is known by its fruits," Wesley insisted that the one desire of "a Methodist" was single-minded devotion to the will of

God. In a Christian world dogged by vicious attacks on other groups of believers, Wesley was emphatic that in maintaining fellowship, Methodists ask only one question: "Do you love and serve God?"

Also published in 1742, *The Principles of a Methodist* was a reply to Josiah Tucker's *A Brief History of the Principles of Methodism*. Josiah Tucker (1712-1799) was an Anglican priest from Bristol. A scholar and noted economic theorist, Tucker was a formidable foe who argued that Wesley's theology was inconsistent, that he believed in sinless perfection and that he was unduly dependent on William Law and the Moravians. In his response, Wesley carefully laid out his full teaching on justification and Christian Perfection. He denied his dependence on Law and the Moravians. Insisting that he believed in justification by faith and rejected sinless perfection, Wesley took great pains to distinguish his actual beliefs about the nature and extent of salvation from the false picture drawn by Tucker. Again, Wesley argued that his teaching on the reality of full salvation was Scriptural and logical. In fact, it was merely that one should love God with all one's heart and one's neighbor as oneself.

Published in 1746, *The Principles of a Methodist Farther Explained* was a response to Thomas Church's *Some Further Remarks on the Rev. Mr. John Wesley's Last Journal*. The title is somewhat confusing, since Wesley is no longer responding to Josiah Tucker. The work is an important defense of Wesley's teaching concerning justification by faith. Again, it is a model of restrained and respectful debate on contested points of Christian doctrine.

—William Kostlevy
Asbury Theological Seminary

Preface

SOMETIMES IT SEEMS THAT we live in the most corrupt age in history, but John Wesley would probably not have seen a great difference between his time and ours. His was a loose, immoral, licentious, violent, skeptical day, and Western civilization was in grave danger of losing its Christian foundation.

Wesley was extremely concerned that Methodists not be seen as adding to the Gospel. He was careful to stress that a holiness believer was not a Dissenter, but rather subscribed to the *whole* Gospel as declared by the Church. He wanted the Bands to be seen, not as a rebellious alternative to established doctrine, but as supportive; not a parachurch organization, but a bolstering, leavening group within it. His was not a theology of the distant, contemplative monastery. He insisted that believers must live out their holiness in everyday life, that testimony would be borne out by behavior.

Following the custom of his time, we cannot look to some topical index in this book, *Holiness in the Midst of Everyday Life,* to find his "take" on a subject. However, by reading the book carefully, we find the logical and scriptural bases for his beliefs, and the source of strength for those who heed his call — then and now — to holiness.

If Wesley walked down the streets of New York or London or Toronto today, he would say there is no difference between the requirements of his day and ours. In Wesley's view, Perfect Love automatically affects the way we interact with our fellowman. It influences the way we price and pay for our goods and services, pay our taxes, give to the poor. It alters the manner in which we seek recreation and how we treat our family members.

It holds sway over everyday life.

Above all, he insisted that the doctrine of the holiness people of his day (the Methodists) was nothing more nor less than the fulfillment of the two greatest commandments of scripture — that we should "love the Lord our God with all our heart, soul, mind and strength, and our neighbor as ourself."

In so doing, we live the life of "holiness in the midst of everyday life."

—D. CURTIS HALE
Publisher

PART I:
THE CHARACTER OF A METHODIST

"Not as though I had already attained."—Philippians 3:12

To The Reader

1. SINCE THE NAME FIRST came abroad into the world, many have been at a loss to know what a Methodist is. What are the principles and the practice of those who are commonly called by that name; and what the distinguishing marks of this sect, "which is everywhere spoken against."

2. And it being generally believed, that I was able to give the clearest account of these things, (as having been one of the first to whom that name was given, and the person by whom the rest were supposed to be directed) I have been called upon, in all manner of ways, and with the utmost earnestness, so to do. I yield at last to the continued insistence both of friends and enemies; and do now give the clearest account I can, in the presence of the Lord and Judge of heaven and earth, of the principles and practice whereby those who are called Methodists are distinguished from other men.

3. I say those who are called Methodists, for let it be well observed, that this is not a name which they take to themselves, but one fixed upon them by way of reproach, without their approbation or consent. It was first given to three or four young men at Oxford, by a student of Christ Church; either in allusion to the ancient sect of Physicians so called, from their teaching, that almost all diseases might be cured by a specific *method* of diet and exercise, or from their observing a more regular *method* of study and behavior than was usual with those of their age and station.

4. I should rejoice (so little ambitious am I to be at the head of any sect or party) if the very name might never be mentioned more, but be buried in eternal oblivion. But if that cannot be, at least let those who will use it know the meaning of the word they use. Let us not always be fighting in the dark. Come, and let us look one another in the face. And perhaps some of you who hate what I am *called*, may love what I *am* by the grace of God; or rather, what "I follow after, if that I may apprehend that for which also I am apprehended of Christ Jesus."

1. THE DISTINGUISHING TRAITS OF a Methodist are not his opinions of any sort. His assenting to this or that scheme of religion, his embracing any particular set of notions, his espousing the judgment of one man or of another, are all quite wide of the point. Whoever, therefore, imagines that a Methodist is a man of such or such an opinion, is grossly ignorant of the whole affair; he mistakes the truth totally. We believe, indeed, that "all Scripture is given by the inspiration of God," and herein we are distinguished from Jews, Turks, and Infidels.

We believe the written Word of God to be the only and sufficient rule both of Christian faith and practice. Herein we are fundamentally distinguished from those of the Romish Church.

We believe Christ to be the eternal, supreme God. Herein we are distinguished from the Socinians and Arians. But as to all opinions which do not strike at the root of Christianity, we think and let think. So that whatsoever they are, whether right or wrong, they are not distinguishing marks of a Methodist.

2. Neither are words or phrases of any sort. We do not place our religion, or any part of it, in being attached to any peculiar mode of speaking, any quaint or uncommon set of expressions. The most obvious, easy, common words, wherein our meaning can be conveyed, we prefer before others, both on ordinary occasions, and when we speak of the things of God. We never, therefore, willingly or designedly, deviate from the most usual way of speaking, unless when we express scripture truths in scripture words, which, we presume, no Christian will condemn. Neither do we affect to use any particular expressions of Scripture more frequently than others, unless they are such as are more frequently used by the inspired writers themselves. So that it is as gross an error, to place the traits of a Methodist in his words, as in opinions of any sort.

3. Nor do we desire to be distinguished by actions, customs, or usages of an indifferent nature. Our religion does not lie in doing what God has not commanded, or abstaining from what he has not

forbidden. It does not lie in the form of our clothing, in the posture of our body, or the covering of our heads. It is not in abstaining from marriage, or from meats and drinks, which are all good if received with thanksgiving. Therefore, neither will any man, who knows what he affirms, fix the trait of a Methodist here— in any actions or customs purely indifferent, undetermined by the word of God.

4. Nor, lastly, is he distinguished by laying the whole stress of religion on any single part of it. If you say, "Yes, he is, for he thinks 'we are saved by faith alone,'" I answer, You do not understand the terms. By salvation he means holiness of heart and life. And this he affirms to spring from true faith alone. Can even a nominal Christian deny it? Is this placing a part of religion for the whole? "Do we then make void the law through faith? God forbid! Yes, we establish the law."

We do not place the whole of religion (as too many do, God knows) either in doing no harm, or in doing good, or in using the ordinances of God. No, not in all of them together; wherein we know by experience a man may labor many years, and at the end have no religion at all, no more than he had at the beginning. Much less in any one of these, or, it may be, in a scrap of one of them. Like her who fancies herself a virtuous woman, only because she is not a prostitute; or him who dreams he is an honest man, merely because he does not rob or steal. May the Lord God of my fathers preserve me from such a poor, starved religion as this! Were this the mark of a Methodist, I would sooner choose to be a sincere Jew, Turk, or Pagan.

5. "What then is the distinguishing trait? Who is a Methodist, according to your own account?" I answer: A Methodist is one who has "the love of God shed abroad in his heart by the Holy Ghost given unto him," one who "loves the Lord his God with all his heart, and with all his soul, and with all his mind, and with all his strength." God is the joy of his heart, and the desire of his soul, which is constantly crying out, "Whom have I in heaven but thee? and there is none upon earth that I desire beside thee! My God and my all! Thou art the strength of my heart, and my portion for ever!"

6. He is therefore happy in God, yes, always happy, as having in him "a well of water springing up into everlasting life," and overflowing

his soul with peace and joy. "Perfect love" having now "cast out fear," he "rejoices evermore." He "rejoices in the Lord always," even "in God his Saviour," and in the Father, "through our Lord Jesus Christ, by whom he hath now received the atonement." "Having" found "redemption through his blood, the forgiveness of his sins," he cannot but rejoice, whenever he looks back on the horrible pit out of which he is delivered. He sees "all his transgressions blotted out as a cloud, and his iniquities as a thick cloud." He cannot but rejoice, whenever he looks on the state wherein he now is, "being justified freely, and having peace with God through our Lord Jesus Christ." For "he that believeth, hath the witness" of this "in himself," being now the son of God by faith. "Because he is a son, God hath sent forth the Spirit of his Son into his heart, crying, Abba, Father!" And "the Spirit itself beareth witness with his spirit, that he is a child of God."

He rejoices also, whenever he looks forward, "in hope of the glory that shall be revealed." Yes, his joy is full, and all his bones cry out, "Blessed be the God and Father of our Lord Jesus Christ, who, according to his abundant mercy, has begotten me again to a living hope — of an inheritance incorruptible, undefiled, and that fades not away, reserved in heaven for me!"

7. And he who has this hope, thus "full of immortality, in everything gives thanks," as knowing that this (whatsoever it is) "is the will of God in Christ Jesus concerning him." From him, therefore, he cheerfully receives all, saying, "Good is the will of the Lord," and whether the Lord gives or takes away, equally "blessing the name of the Lord." For he has "learned, in whatsoever state he is, therewith to be content." He knows "both how to be abased and how to abound. Everywhere and in all things he is instructed both to be full and to be hungry, both to abound and suffer need." Whether in ease or pain, whether in sickness or health, whether in life or death, he gives thanks from the ground of his heart to Him who orders it for good. He knows that as "every good gift cometh from above," so none but good can come from the Father of Lights, into whose hand he has wholly committed his body and soul, as into the hands of a faithful Creator. He is therefore "careful" (anxious or uneasy) "for nothing;" as having "cast all his care on Him that careth for him," and "in all

things" resting on him, after "making his request known to him with thanksgiving."

8. He "prays without ceasing." It is given him "always to pray, and not to faint." Not that he is always in the house of prayer, though he neglects no opportunity of being there. Neither is he always on his knees, although he often is, or on his face, before the Lord his God. Nor yet is he always crying aloud to God, or calling upon him in words. Many times "the Spirit maketh intercession for him with groans that cannot be uttered." But at all times the language of his heart is this: "Thou brightness of the eternal glory, unto you is my heart, though without a voice, and my silence speaks unto you." And this is true prayer, and this alone. But his heart is ever lifted up to God, at all times and in all places. In this he is never hindered, much less interrupted, by any person or thing. In private or company, in leisure, business, or conversation, his heart is ever with the Lord. Whether he lie down or rise up, God is in all his thoughts. He walks with God continually, having the loving eye of his mind still fixed upon him, and everywhere "seeing Him that is invisible."

9. And while he thus always exercises his love to God, by praying without ceasing, rejoicing evermore, and in everything giving thanks, this commandment is written in his heart, "That he who loves God, loves his brother also." He accordingly loves his neighbor as himself. He loves every man as his own soul. His heart is full of love to all mankind, to every child of "the Father of the spirits of all flesh." That a man is not personally known to him is no bar to his love — no, nor that he is known to be such as he does not approve, that he repays hatred for his goodwill. He "loves his enemies," yes, and the enemies of God, "the evil and the unthankful." If it is not in his power to "do good to them that hate him," yet he ceases not to pray for them, though they continue to spurn his love, and still "despitefully use him and persecute him."

10. He is "pure in heart." The love of God has purified his heart from all revengeful passions, from envy, malice, and wrath, from every unkind temper or malign emotion. It has cleansed him from pride and haughtiness of spirit, from which alone comes contention. He has now "put on bowels of mercies, kindness, humbleness of mind, meekness, longsuffering." He "forbears and forgives, if he

had a quarrel against any; even as God in Christ hath forgiven him." Indeed all possible ground for contention on his part is utterly cut off. None can take from him what he desires, seeing he "loves not the world, nor" any of "the things of the world," being now "crucified to the world, and the world crucified to him." He is dead to all that is in the world, both to "the lust of the flesh, the lust of the eye, and the pride of life." For "all his desire is unto God, and to the remembrance of his name."

11. Agreeable to this his one desire, is the one design of his life, namely, "not to do his own will, but the will of Him that sent him." His one intention at all times and in all things is not to please himself, but Him whom his soul loves. He has a single eye. And because "his eye is single, his whole body is full of light." Indeed, where the loving eye of the soul is continually fixed upon God, there can be no darkness at all, "but the whole is light; as when the bright shining of a candle enlightens the house." God then reigns alone. All that is in the soul is holiness to the Lord. There is not a motion in his heart but is according to his will. Every thought that arises points to Him, and is in obedience to the law of Christ.

12. The tree is known by its fruits. As he loves God, so he keeps his commandments; not only some, or most of them, but all, from the least to the greatest. He is not content to "keep the whole law, and offend in one point," but has in all points, "a conscience void of offence towards God and towards man." Whatever God has forbidden, he avoids. Whatever God has commanded, he does, whether it is little or great, hard or easy, joyous or grievous to the flesh. He "runs the way of God's commandments," now he has set his heart at liberty. It is his glory to do so. It is his daily crown of rejoicing "to do the will of God on earth, as it is done in heaven." He knows it is the highest privilege of "the angels of God, of those that excel in strength, to fulfil his commandments, and listen to the voice of his word."

13. All the commandments of God he accordingly keeps, and that with all his might. For his obedience is in proportion to his love, the source from which it flows. Therefore, loving God with all his heart, he serves him with all his strength. He continually presents his soul and body a living sacrifice, holy, acceptable to God; entirely and

without reserve devoting himself, all he has, and all he is, to his glory. All the talents he has received, he constantly employs according to his Master's will; every power and faculty of his soul, every member of his body. Once he "yielded" them "unto sin" and the devil, "as instruments of unrighteousness." But now, "being alive from the dead, he yields" them all "as instruments of righteousness unto God."

14. By consequence, whatever he does, it is all to the glory of God. In all his work of every kind, he not only aims at this (which is implied in having a single eye) but actually attains it. His business and refreshments, as well as his prayers, all serve this great end. Whether he sits in his house or walks by the way, whether he lie down or rise up, he is promoting, in all he speaks or does, the one business of his life. Whether he puts on his clothes, or labors, or eats and drinks, or diverts himself from tiring labor, it all tends to advance the glory of God, by peace and goodwill among men. His one invariable rule is this: "Whatsoever ye do, in word or deed, do it all in the name of the Lord Jesus, giving thanks to God and the Father by him."

15. Nor do the customs of the world at all hinder his "running the race that is set before him." He knows that vice does not lose its nature, though it becomes ever so fashionable, and remembers, that "every man is to give an account of himself to God." He cannot, therefore, "follow" even "a multitude to do evil." He cannot "fare sumptuously every day," or "make provision for the flesh to fulfil the lusts thereof." He cannot "lay up treasures upon earth," any more than he can take fire into his bosom. He cannot "adorn himself," on any pretence, "with gold or costly apparel."

He cannot join in or tolerate any recreation which has the least tendency to vice of any kind. He cannot "speak evil" of his neighbor, any more than he can lie either for God or man. He cannot utter an unkind word of anyone, for love keeps the door of his lips. He cannot speak "idle words." "No corrupt communication" ever "comes out of his mouth," as is all that "which is" not "good to the use of edifying," not "fit to minister grace to the hearers." But "whatsoever things are pure, whatsoever things are lovely, whatsoever things are" justly "of good report," he thinks, and speaks, and acts, "adorning the Gospel of our Lord Jesus Christ in all things."

16. Lastly: As he has time, he "does good unto all men," to neighbors and strangers, friends and enemies, and that in every possible kind; not only to their bodies, by "feeding the hungry, clothing the naked, visiting those that are sick or in prison," but much more does he labor to do good to their souls, as of the ability which God gives. He labors to awaken those that sleep in death; to bring those who are awakened to the atoning blood, that, "being justified by faith, they may have peace with God," and to provoke those who have peace with God to abound more in love and in good works. He is willing to "spend and be spent herein," even "to be offered up on the sacrifice and service of their faith," so they may "all come to the measure of the stature of the fullness of Christ."

17. These are the principles and practices of our sect. These are the traits of a true Methodist. By these alone do those who are in derision desire to be distinguished from other men. If any man say, "Why, these are only the common fundamental principles of Christianity!" you have said. So I mean; this is the very truth. I know they are not otherwise.

And I would to God both you and all men knew, that I and all who follow my judgment vehemently refuse to be distinguished from other men by any but the common principles of Christianity—the plain, old Christianity that I teach, renouncing and detesting all other marks of distinction.

And whoever is what I preach (let him be called what he will, for names change not the nature of things) he is a Christian, not in name only, but in heart and in life. He is inwardly and outwardly conformed to the will of God, as revealed in the written Word. He thinks, speaks, and lives, according to the method laid down in the revelation of Jesus Christ. His soul is renewed after the image of God, in righteousness and in all true holiness. And having the mind that was in Christ, he so walks as Christ also walked.

18. By these traits, by these fruits of a living faith, do we labor to distinguish ourselves from the unbelieving world, from all those whose minds or lives are not according to the Gospel of Christ. But from real Christians, of whatsoever denomination they be, we earnestly desire not to be distinguished at all, not from any who sincerely follow after what they know they have not yet attained. No,

"whosoever doeth the will of my Father which is in heaven, the same is my brother, and sister, and mother."

I plead with you, brethren, by the mercies of God, that we be in no way divided among ourselves. Is your heart right, as my heart is with yours? I ask no further question. If it is, give me your hand. For opinions or terms let us not destroy the work of God.

Do you love and serve God? It is enough. I give you the right hand of fellowship. If there is any consolation in Christ, if any comfort of love, if any fellowship of the Spirit, if any innermost parts and mercies, let us strive together for the faith of the Gospel. Let us walk worthy of the vocation wherewith we are called; with all lowliness and meekness, with longsuffering, forbearing one another in love, endeavoring to keep the unity of the Spirit in the bond of peace. Let us remember, there is one body, and one Spirit, even as we are called with one hope of our calling, "one Lord, one faith, one baptism; one God and Father of all, who is above all, and through all, and in you all."

The Whole Armor of God (Ephesians 6)

1. Soldiers of Christ, arise,
    And put your Armor on,
Strong in the Strength which God supplies
    Thro' his Eternal Son;
Strong in the Lord of Hosts,
    And in his mighty Power,
Who in the Strength of Jesus trusts
    Is more than Conqueror.

2. Stand then in His great Might,
    With all his Strength endu'd,
And take, to arm you for the Fight,
    The Panoply of God;
That having all Things done,
    And all your Conflicts past,
Ye may o'ercome thro' Christ alone,
    And stand entire at last.

3. Stand then against your Foes,
    In close and firm array,
Legions of wily Fiends oppose
    Throughout the Evil Day;
But meet the Sons of Night
    But mock their vain Design,
Arm'd in the Arms of Heavenly Light
    In Righteousness Divine.

4. Leave no unguarded Place,
    No Weakness of the Soul,
Take every Virtue, every Grace,
    And fortify the whole,
Indissolubly join'd,
    To Battle all proceed,
But arm yourselves with all the Mind
    That was in Christ your Head.

5. Let Truth the Girdle be
    That binds your Armor on,
In faithful firm Sincerity
    To Jesus cleave alone;
Let Faith and Love combine
    To guard your Valiant Breast,
The Plate be Righteousness Divine,
    Imputed and Imprest.

6. Still let your Feet be shod,
    Ready His Will to do,
Ready in all the Ways of God
    His Glory to pursue;
Ruin is spread beneath,
    The Gospel greaves put on,
And safe thro' all the snares of Death
    To Life eternal run.

7. But above all, lay hold
    On Faith's victorious Shield,
Arm'd with that Adamant and Gold
    Be sure to win the Field;
If Faith surround your Heart,
    Satan shall be subdu'd,
Repell'd his every Fiery Dart,
    And quench'd with Jesu's Blood.

8. Jesus hath died for you!
    What can his Love withstand?
Believe; hold fast your Shield; and who
    Shalt pluck you from His Hand?
Believe that Jesus reigns,
    All Power to Him is giv'n,
Believe, 'till freed from Sin's remains,
    Believe yourselves to Heaven.

9. Your Rock can never shake:
    Hither, He saith, come up!
The Helmet of Salvation take,
    The Confidence of Hope:
Hope, for His Perfect Love,
    Hope for His People's Rest,
Hope to sit down with Christ above
    And Share the Marriage Feast.

10. Brandish in Faith 'till then
    The Spirit's two-edg'd Sword,
Hew all the Share of Fiends and Men
    In pieces with the Word;
'Tis written; This applied
    Baffles their Strength and Art;
Spirit and Soul with this divide,
And Joints and Marrow part.

11. To keep your Armor bright
    Attend with constant Care,
Still walking in your Captain's Sight,
    And watching unto Prayer;
Ready for all Alarms,
    Steadfastly set your Face,
And always exercise your Arms,
    And use your every Grace.

12. Pray without ceasing pray,
    (Your Captain gives the Word)
His Summons cheerfully obey,
    And call upon the Lord;
To God your every Want
    In Instant Prayer display,
Pray always; pray, and never faint;
    Pray, without ceasing pray.

13. In Fellowship; alone
    To God with Faith draw near,
Approach his Courts, besiege his Throne
    With all the Power of Prayer;
Go to his Temple, go,
    Nor from his Altar move;
Let every house His Worship know;
    And every Heart His Love.

14. To God your Spirits dart,
    Your Souls in Words declare,
Or groan, to him who reads the Heart,
    Th' unutterable Prayer.
His Mercy now implore,
    And now show forth his praise,
In Shouts, or silent Awe adore,
    His Miracles of Grace.

15. Pour out your Souls to God,
    And bow them with your Knees,
And spread your Hearts and Hands abroad,
    And pray for Sion's *Peace;*
Your Guides and Brethren, bear
    Forever on your Mind;
Extend the Arms of mighty Prayer
    Ingrasping all Mankind.

16. From Strength to Strength go on,
    Wrestle, and fight, and pray,
Tread all the Powers of Darkness down,
    And win the well-fought Day;
Still let the Spirit cry
    In all His Soldiers, "Come."
Till Christ the Lord Descends from High,
    And takes the Conqu'rors Home.

PART II:
THE PRINCIPLES OF A METHODIST

Occasioned by a late Pamphlet, entitled,
"A Brief History of the Principles of Methodism"

To The Reader

1. I HAVE OFTEN WRITTEN on controverted points before, but not with an eye to any particular person. This is the first time I have appeared in controversy, properly so called. Indeed I have not wanted occasion to do it before, particularly when, after many stabs in the dark, I was publicly attacked, not by an open enemy, but by my own familiar friend. But I could not answer him. I could only cover my face and say, *Και συ εις εκεινων; Και συ, τεκνον*; "Are you also among them? Are you, my son?"

2. I now tread an untried path "with fear and trembling," fear, not of my adversary, but of myself. I fear my own spirit, lest I "fall where many mightier have been slain." I never knew one man (or but one) write controversy, with what I thought a right spirit. Every disputant seems to think (as every soldier) that he may hurt his opponent as much as he can— no, that he ought to do his worst to him — or he cannot make the best of his own cause. So long as he does not belie or willfully misrepresent him, he must expose him as far as he is able. It is enough, we suppose, if we do not show heat or passion against our adversary. But, not to despise him, or endeavor to make others do so, is quite a work uncalled-for.

3. But ought these things to be so? (I speak on the Christian scheme.) Ought we not to love our neighbor as ourselves? Does a man cease to be our neighbor, because he is of a different opinion; oh no, and declares himself so to be? Ought we not, for all this, to do to him as we would he should do to us? But do we ourselves love to be exposed, or set in the worst light? Would we willingly be treated with contempt? If not, why do we treat others thus? And yet who scruples it? Who does not hit every blow he can, however foreign to the merits of the cause? Who, in controversy, casts the mantle of love over the nakedness of his brother? Who keeps steadily and uniformly to the question, without ever striking at the person? Who shows, in every sentence, that he loves his brother only less than the truth?

4. I have made a little faint essay toward this. I have a brother

who is as my own soul. My desire is, in every word I say, to look upon Mr. Tucker as in his place, and to speak not one tittle concerning the one in any other spirit than I would speak concerning the other.

Whether I have attained this or not, I do not know, for my heart is "deceitful and desperately wicked." If I have spoken anything in another spirit, I pray God it may not be laid to my charge, and that it may not condemn me in that day when the secrets of all hearts shall be made manifest!

Meanwhile, my heart's desire and prayer to God is, that both I, and all who think it their duty to oppose me, may "put on bowels of mercies, kindness, humbleness of mind, meekness, longsuffering; forbearing one another, and forgiving one another, even as God for Christ's sake has forgiven us."

1. THERE HAS LATELY APPEARED in the world a tract, entitled, *A Brief History of the Principles of Methodism*. I doubt not but the writer's design was good, and believe he has a real desire to know the truth. The manner wherein he pursues that design is generally calm and dispassionate. He is, indeed, in several mistakes, but as many of these are either of small consequence in themselves, or do not immediately relate to me, it is not my concern to mention them. All of any consequence which relates to me, I think, falls under three topics:

First: That I believe justification by faith alone.

Secondly: That I believe sinless perfection. And,

Thirdly: That I believe inconsistencies.

Of each of these I will speak as plainly as I can.

2. First. That I believe justification by faith alone. This I allow. I am firmly persuaded, that every man of the offspring of Adam is very far gone from original righteousness, and is of his own nature inclined to evil. This corruption of our nature, in every person born into the world, deserves God's wrath and damnation.Therefore, if ever we receive the remission of our sins, and are accounted righteous before God, it must be only for the merit of Christ by faith, and not for our own works or deserving of any kind. No, I am persuaded, that all works done before justification, have in them the nature of sin. Consequently, till he is justified, a man has no power to do any work which is pleasing and acceptable to God.

3. To express my meaning a little more at large: I believe three things must go together in our justification. Upon God's part is his great mercy and grace. Upon Christ's part is the satisfaction of God's justice, by offering his body and shedding his blood. Upon our part is true and living faith in the merits of Jesus Christ. In our justification there is not only God's mercy and grace, but his justice also. The grace of God does not shut out the righteousness of God in our justification, but only shuts out the

righteousness of man, that is, the righteousness of our works.

4. And therefore St. Paul requires nothing on the part of man, but only a true and living faith. Yet this faith does not shut out repentance, hope, and love, which are joined with faith in every man that is justified. But it shuts them out from the office of justifying. Although they are all present together in him that is justified, yet they justify not all together.

5. Neither does faith shut out good works, necessarily, to be done afterwards. But we may not do them to be justified by doing them. Our justification comes freely, of the mere mercy of God. As all the world was not able to pay any part towards their ransom, it pleased him, without any of our deserving, to prepare for us Christ's body and blood, whereby our ransom might be paid, and his justice satisfied. Christ, therefore, is now the righteousness of all them that truly believe in him.

6. But let it be observed, the true sense of those words, "We are justified by faith in Christ only," is not, that our own act—"to believe in Christ"—or our faith which is within us, justifies us. That were to account ourselves to be justified by some act or virtue that is within us. Although we have faith, hope, and love within us, and do never so many good works, yet we must renounce the merit of all, of faith, hope, love, and all other virtues and good works, which we either have done, shall do, or can do, as far too weak to deserve our justification. Therefore, we must trust only in God's mercy, and the merits of Christ, for it is he alone that takes away our sins. To him alone are we to go for this, forsaking all our virtues, good words, thoughts, and works, and putting our trust in Christ only.

7. In strictness, therefore, neither our faith nor our works justify us, that is, deserve the remission of our sins. But God himself justifies us, of his own mercy, through the merits of his Son only. Nevertheless, because by faith we embrace the promise of God's mercy and of the remission of our sins, therefore the Scripture says, that faith does justify, yes, faith without works.

It is all one to say, "Faith without works," and "Faith alone, justifies us." Therefore the ancient Fathers from time to time speak thus: "Faith alone justifies us." We receive faith through the only merits of Christ, and not through the merit and virtue we have, or work we do. Therefore in that respect we renounce, as it were, again, faith, works, and all other virtues. Our corruption through original sin is so great that all our faith, charity, words, and works cannot merit or deserve any part of our justification for us. Therefore we thus speak, humbling ourselves before God, and giving Christ all the glory of our justification.

8. But it should also be observed, what that faith is by which we are justified. Now, that faith which brings not forth good works is not a living faith, but a dead and devilish one. For even the devils believe that Christ was born of a virgin; that he wrought all kinds of miracles, declaring himself to be very God; that for our sakes he died and rose again, and ascended into heaven; and at the end of the world shall come again, to judge the quick and the dead. This the devils believe, and so they believe all that is written in the Old and New Testament. Still, for all this faith, they are but devils. They remain still in their damnable estate, lacking the true Christian faith.

9. The true Christian faith is, not only to believe that the Holy Scriptures and the articles of our faith are true; but also, to have "a sure trust and confidence to be saved from everlasting damnation by Christ," which is followed by a loving heart, to obey his commandments. And this faith neither any devil has, nor any wicked man. No ungodly man has or can have this "sure trust and confidence in God, that by the merits of Christ his sins are forgiven, and he is reconciled to the favour of God."

10. This is what I believe (and have believed for some years) concerning justification by faith alone. I have chosen to express it in the words of a little treatise, published several years ago, as being the most authentic proof, both of my past and present sentiments. If I err herein, let those who are better informed calmly point out my error to me. I trust I shall not shut my eyes against the light, from whatever side it comes.

11. The second thing laid to my charge is that I believe sinless perfection. I will simply declare what I do believe concerning this also, and leave unprejudiced men to judge.

12. My last and most deliberate thoughts on this topic were published but a few months since, in these words:

(a.) "Perhaps the general prejudice against Christian perfection may chiefly arise from a misapprehension of the nature of it. We willingly allow, and continually declare, there is no such perfection in this life. This implies either a release from doing good and attending all the ordinances of God; or a freedom from ignorance, mistake, temptation, and a thousand infirmities necessarily connected with flesh and blood.

(b.) "First. We not only allow, but earnestly contend, that there is no perfection in this life, which implies any release from attending all the ordinances of God, or from 'doing good unto all men, while we have time,' though 'specially unto the household of faith.' We believe that not only the babes in Christ, who have newly found redemption in his blood, but those also who are 'grown up into perfect men,' are indispensably obliged, as often as they have opportunity, 'to eat bread and drink wine in remembrance of Him,' and to 'search the Scriptures.' By fasting, as well as temperance, they should 'keep their bodies under, and bring them into subjection.' Above all, they should pour out their souls in prayer, both secretly and in the great congregation.

(c.) "We, secondly, believe that there is no such perfection in this life as implies an entire deliverance, either from ignorance or mistake, in things not essential to salvation, or from manifold temptations, or from numberless infirmities by which the corruptible body more or less presses down the soul. We cannot find any ground in Scripture to suppose that any inhabitant of a house of clay is wholly exempt, either from bodily infirmities or from ignorance of many things, or to imagine anyone is incapable of mistake, or falling into various temptations.

(d.) "'But whom then do you mean by one that is perfect?' We mean one in whom 'is the mind which was in Christ,' and who so 'walketh as Christ walked.' We mean a 'man that has clean hands and a pure heart,' or that is 'cleansed from all filthiness of flesh and spirit;' one in whom 'is no occasion of stumbling,' and who accordingly 'does not commit sin.'

To declare this a little more particularly: We understand by that scriptural expression, 'a perfect man,' one in whom God has fulfilled his faithful word, 'From all your filthiness and from all your idols will I cleanse you: I will also save you from all your uncleanness.' We understand hereby one whom God has 'sanctified throughout, in body, soul, and spirit;' one who 'walketh in the light as he is in the light, in whom is no darkness at all; the blood of Jesus Christ his Son having cleansed him from all sin.'

(e.) "This man can now testify to all mankind, 'I am crucified with Christ: Nevertheless I live; yet not I, but Christ liveth in me.' He is 'holy, as God who called him is holy,' both in heart and 'in all manner of conversation.' He 'loveth the Lord his God with all his heart,' and serves him 'with all his strength.' He 'loveth his neighbor,' every man, 'as himself,' yes, 'as Christ loved us.' He loves them, in particular, that 'despitefully use him and persecute him, because they know not the Son, neither the Father.' Indeed his soul is all love, filled with 'bowels of mercies, kindness, meekness, gentleness, long-suffering.' And his life agrees thereto, full of 'the work of faith, the patience of hope, the labor of love. And whatsoever he doeth either in word or deed, he doeth it all in the name,' in the love and power, 'of the Lord Jesus.' In a word, he does 'the will of God on earth, as it is done in heaven.'

(f.) "This it is to be 'a perfect man,' to be sanctified throughout: Even 'to have a heart so all-flaming with the love of God'—to use Archbishop Usher's words—'as continually to offer up every thought, word, and work, as a spiritual sacrifice, acceptable to God through Christ.' In every thought of our hearts, in every word of our tongues, in every work of our hands, to 'show forth his praise, who hath called us out of darkness into his marvelous light.' Oh, that both we and all who seek the Lord Jesus in sincerity, may thus be made perfect in one!'"

13. If there is anything unscriptural in these words, anything wild or extravagant, anything contrary to the analogy of faith, or the experience of adult Christians, let them "smite me friendly and reprove me." Let them share with me the clearer light God has given them. How do you know, Oh man, "but you may gain your brother," but he may at length come to the knowledge of the truth; and your labor of love, shown with meekness of wisdom, may not be in vain?

14. There remains yet another charge against me, that I believe inconsistencies; that my tenets, particularly concerning justification, are contradictory to themselves; that Mr. Wesley, "since his return

from Germany, has improved in the spirit of inconsistency." "For then he published two treatises of Dr. Barnes, the Calvinist, or Dominican rather, who suffered in 1541; [Let us spare the ashes of the dead. Were I such a Dominican as he was, I should rejoice too to die in the flames.] the first on "Justification by faith only;" the other on "the sinfulness of man's natural will, and his utter inability to do works acceptable to God, until he be justified." Which principles, if added to his former tenets [Oh, no, they need not be *added to* them, for they are the very same] will give the whole a new vein of inconsistency, and make the contradictions more gross and glaring than before.

15. It will be necessary to speak more largely on this topic than on either of the preceding. In order to speak as distinctly as I can, I propose taking the paragraphs one by one, as they lie before me.

16. (a.) It is "asserted that Mr. Law's system was the creed of the Methodists." But it is not proved. I had been eight years at Oxford before I read any of Mr. Law's writings. When I did, I was so far from making them my creed that I had objections to almost every page. But all this time my manner was, to spend several hours a day in reading the Scripture in the original tongues. From here my system, so termed, was wholly drawn, according to the light I then had.

17. In my passage to Georgia, I met with those teachers who would have taught me the way of God more perfectly, but I understood them not. Neither, on my arrival there, did they infuse any particularities into me, either about justification or anything else. I came back with the same notions I went. I have explicitly acknowledged this in my second *Journal*, where some of my words are these: "When Peter Böhler, as soon as I came to London, affirmed of true faith in Christ (which is but one) that it had these two fruits inseparably attending it, 'dominion over sin, and constant peace from a sense of forgiveness,' I was quite amazed, and looked upon it as a new gospel. If this was so, it was clear I had no faith, but I was not willing to be convinced of this. Therefore I disputed with all my might, and labored to prove that faith might be where these were not, especially where that sense of forgiveness was not. For all the scriptures relating to this I had been long since taught to construe

away, and to call all Presbyterians who spoke otherwise. Besides, I well saw, no one could (in the nature of things) have such a sense of forgiveness, and not feel it. But I felt it not. If then there was no faith without this, all my pretensions to faith dropped at once." (*Vol. I. p. 101.*)

18. (b.) Yet it was not Peter Böhler who convinced me that conversion (I mean justification) was an instantaneous work. On the contrary, when I was convinced of the nature and fruits of justifying faith, still "I could not comprehend what he spoke of an instantaneous work. I could not understand how this faith should be given in a moment; how a man could at once be thus turned from darkness to light, from sin and misery to righteousness and joy in the Holy Ghost. I searched the Scriptures again, touching this very thing, particularly the Acts of the Apostles. But to my utter astonishment, I found scarce any instances there of other than instantaneous conversions; scarce any others so slow as that of St. Paul, who was three days in the pangs of the new birth. I had but one retreat left, *viz.*, 'Thus, I grant, God worked in the first ages of Christianity. But the times are changed. What reason have I to believe he works in the same manner now?'

"But on Sunday, 23, I was beat out of this retreat too, by the concurring evidence of several living witnesses, who testified God had thus worked in themselves, giving them *in a moment* such a faith in the blood of his Son as translated them out of darkness into light, out of sin and fear into holiness and happiness. Here ended my disputing. I could now only cry out, 'Lord, help my unbelief!'" (*Vol. I. p. 91.*) The remaining part of this section, with the third and fourth, contain my own words, to which I still subscribe.

And if there is a mistake in the fifth, it is not material.

19. (c.) It is true, that "on Wednesday, July 12, the Count spoke to this effect:

"(1.) Justification is the forgiveness of sins.

"(2.) The moment a man flies to Christ, he is justified.

"(3.) And has peace with God, but not always joy.

"(4.) Nor perhaps may he know he is justified till long after.

"(5.) For the assurance of it is distinct from justification itself.

"(6.) But others may know he is justified, by his power over sin, by his seriousness, his love of the brethren, and his hunger and thirst after righteousness; which alone proves the spiritual life to be begun.

"(7.) To be justified is the same thing as to be born of God. When a man is awakened, he is begotten of God, and his fear, and sorrow, and sense of the wrath of God, are the pangs of the new birth."

It is true also, that I then recollected what P. Böhler had often said on this topic, which was to this effect:

"(1.) When a man has living faith in Christ, then he is justified.

"(2.) This is always given in a moment.

"(3.) And in that moment he has peace with God.

"(4.) Which he cannot have without knowing that he has it.

"(5.) And being born of God, he sins not.

"(6.) Which deliverance from sin he cannot have without knowing that he has it."

21. I did not consider it possible for any man living to have imagined that I believed both these accounts; the words whereof I had purposely so ranged and divided into short sentences, that the gross, irreconcilable difference between them might be plain to the meanest reader. I cannot therefore but be a little surprised at the strength of that prejudice which could prevent anyone's seeing, that, in opposition to the Count's opinion, (which in many respects I wholly disapproved of) I quoted the words of one of his own Church, which if true, overturn it altogether.

22. I have nothing to object to the quotations made in the seventh, eighth, and ninth sections. In the tenth are these words:

"Now, since Mr. Wesley went so far to gather such materials together, let us see what was the system (or rather the medley) of principles he had to return with to England."

"Of the Assurance of Justification

"I believe that conversion is an instantaneous work; and that the moment a man is converted, or has living faith in Christ, he is justified: Which faith a man cannot have, without knowing that he has it.

"Yet I believe he may not know that he is justified (that is, that he has living faith) till a long time after.

"I believe, also, that the moment a man is justified he has peace with God.

"Which he cannot have without knowing that he has it.

"Yet I believe he may not know that he is justified (that is, that he has peace with God) till a long time after.

"I believe when a man is justified he is born of God.

"And being born of God, he sins not.

"Which deliverance from sin he cannot have without knowing it.

"Yet I believe he may not know that he is justified (that is, delivered from sin) till a long time after.

"Though I believe that others may know that he is justified, by his power over sin, his seriousness, and love of the brethren."

"Of the Conditions of Justification

"23. I believe that Christ 'formed in us,' subordinately to Christ 'given for us,' (that is, our own inherent righteousness subordinate to Christ's merits) ought to be insisted upon, as necessary to our justification.

"And it is just and right that a man should be humble and penitent, and have a broken and contrite heart (that is, should have Christ formed in him) before he can expect to be justified.

"And that this penitence and contrition is the work of the Holy Ghost.

"Yet I believe that all this is nothing towards, and has no influence on, our justification.

"Again, I believe that, in order to justification, I must go straight to Christ, with all my ungodliness, and plead nothing else.

"Yet I believe that we should not insist upon anything we do or feel, as if it were necessary *previous* to justification."

"Of the Effects of Justification

"24. I believe that justification is the same thing as to be born of God. Yet a man may have a strong assurance that he is justified, and not be able to affirm that he is born of God.

"A man may be fully assured that his sins are forgiven, yet may not be able to tell the hour or day when he received this full assurance, because it may grow up in him by degrees. Though he can remember that, from the time this full assurance was confirmed in him, he never lost it, no, not for a moment.

"A man may have a weak faith at the same time that he has peace with God, not one uneasy thought, and freedom from sin, not one unholy desire.

"A man may be justified, that is, born of God, who has not a clean heart, that is, is not sanctified.

"He may be justified, that is, born of God, and not have the indwelling of the Spirit."

25. I entirely agree, "that the foregoing creed is a very extraordinary and odd composition," but it is not mine. I neither composed it, nor believe it; as, I doubt not, every impartial reader will be fully convinced, when we shall have gone over it, once more, step by step.

The parts of it which I do believe I shall barely repeat. On the others it will be needful to add a few words.

"Of the Assurance of Justification

"I believe that conversion," meaning thereby justification, "is an instantaneous work; and that the moment a man has living faith in Christ, he is converted or justified." (So the proposition must be expressed for it to make sense.) "Which faith he cannot have, without knowing that he has it."

"Yet I believe he may not know that he has it till long after." This I deny. I believe no such thing.

"I believe the moment a man is justified he has peace with God:

"Which he cannot have without knowing that he has it.

"Yet I believe he may not know he has it till long after." This again I deny. I believe it not, nor does Michael Linner. To clear him entirely, one need only read his own words:

"About fourteen years ago, I was more than ever convinced that I was wholly different from what God required me to be. I consulted his word again and again, but it spoke nothing but condemnation. At last I could not read, nor indeed do anything else, having no hope and no spirit left in me. I had been in this state for several days, when, musing by myself, those words came strongly into my mind, 'God so loved the world that he gave his only begotten Son, to the end that all who believe in him should not perish, but have everlasting life.' I thought, '*All!* Then I am one. Then He is given for *me*. But I am a sinner, and he came to save sinners.' Immediately my burden dropped off, and my heart was at rest.

"But the full assurance of faith I had not yet, nor for the two years I continued in Moravia. When I was driven out of there by the Jesuits, I retired here, and was soon after received into the Church. Here, after some time, it pleased our Lord to manifest himself more clearly to my soul, and give me that full sense of acceptance in him which excludes all doubt and fear.

"Indeed, the leading of the Spirit is different in different souls. His more usual method, I believe, is, to give, in one and the same moment, forgiveness of sins, and a full assurance of that forgiveness. Yet in many he works as he did in me; giving first the remission of sins, and after some weeks, or months, or years, the full assurance of it." (Vol. I. p. 128.)

All I need observe is, that the first sense of forgiveness is often mixed with doubt or fear. But the full assurance of faith excludes all doubt and fear, as the very term implies.

Therefore, instead of, "He may not know that he has peace with God till long after," it should be, (to agree with Michael Linner's words,) "He may not have, till long after, the full assurance of faith, which excludes all doubt and fear."

"I believe a man is justified at the same time that he is born of God.

"And he that is born of God sins not.

"Which deliverance from sin he cannot have, without knowing that he has it."

"Yet I believe he may not know it till long after." This also I utterly deny.

"Of the Conditions of Justification

"26. I believe that Christ 'formed in us' ought to be insisted on, as necessary to our justification."

I no more believe this than Christian David does, whose words concerning it are these:

"It pleased God to show me that Christ in us, and Christ for us, ought to be both insisted on.

"But I clearly saw we ought not to insist on anything we feel, any more than anything we do, as if it were necessary previous to our justification.

"And before a man can expect to be justified, he should be horrible and penitent, and have a broken and contrite heart, that is, should have Christ formed in him." No, that is quite another thing. I believe every man is penitent before he is justified. He repents before he believes the gospel. But it is never before he is justified that Christ is formed in him.

"And that this penitence and contrition is the work of the Holy Ghost.

"Yet I believe that all this is nothing towards, and has no influence on, our justification."

Christian David's words are, "Observe, this is not the foundation. It is not this by which (for the sake of which) you are justified. This is not the righteousness, this is no part of the righteousness, by which you are reconciled to God. You grieve for your sins. You are deeply humbled. Your heart is broken. Well, but all this is nothing to your justification." The words immediately following fix the sense of this otherwise exceptionable sentence. "The remission of your sins is not owing to this cause, either in whole or in part. Your humiliation has no influence on that." Not as a cause, so the very last words explain it.

"Again, I believe that in order to obtain justification, I must go straight to Christ, with all my ungodliness, and plead nothing else."

"Yet I believe we should not insist on anything we do or feel, as if it were necessary previous to justification." No, nor on anything else. So the whole tenor of Christian David's words implies.

Of the Effects of Justification

27. "I believe a man may have a strong assurance he is justified, and not be able to affirm he is a child of God."

Feder's words are these: "I found my heart at rest, in good hope that my sins were forgiven, of which I had a stronger assurance six weeks after. [True, comparatively stronger, though still mixed with doubt and fear.] But I dare not affirm, I am a child of God." I see no inconsistency in all this. Many such instances I know at this day. I myself was one for some time.

"A man may be fully assured that his sins are forgiven, yet may not be able to tell the day when he received this full assurance, because it grew up in him by degrees. [Of this also I know a few other instances.] But from the time this full assurance was confirmed in him, he never lost it." Very true and, I think, consistent.

Neuser's own words are, "In him I found true rest to my soul, being fully assured that all my sins were forgiven. Yet I cannot tell the hour or day when I first received that full assurance. For it was not given me at first, neither at once; [not in its fullness] but grew up in me by degrees. And from the time it was confirmed in me I have never lost it, having never since doubted, no, not for a moment."

"A man may have a weak faith, at the same time that he has peace with God, and no unholy desires."

A man may be justified, who has not a clean heart.

28. Not in the full sense of the word. This I do truly believe is sound divinity, agreeable both to Scripture and experience. And I believe it is consistent with itself. As to the "hundred other absurdities which might be fully and fairly made out," it will be time enough to consider them, when they are produced.

29. But whether I have succeeded in attempting to reconcile these things or not, I truly think Mr. Tucker has. I desire not a more consistent account of my principles, than he has himself given in the following words:

"Our spiritual state should be considered distinctly under each of these views.

"1. Before justification, in which state we may be said to be unable to do any thing acceptable to God. Then we can do nothing but come to Christ, which ought not to be considered as doing anything, but as supplicating (or waiting) to receive a power of doing for the time to come.

"For the preventing grace of God, which is common to all, is sufficient to bring us to Christ, though it is not sufficient to carry us any farther till we are justified.

"2. After justification. The moment a man comes to Christ (by faith) he is justified, and born again. He is born again in the imperfect sense (for there are two [if not more] degrees of regeneration) and he has power over all the stirrings and motions of sin, but not a total freedom from them. Therefore he has not yet, in the full and proper sense, a new and clean heart. But being exposed to various temptations, he may and will fall again from this condition, if he does not attain to a more excellent gift."[1]

3. Sanctification is the last and highest state of perfection in this life, for then are the faithful born again in the full and perfect sense. Then is there given unto them a new and clean heart, and the struggle between the old and new man is over.[2]

30. That I may say many things which have been said before, and perhaps by Calvin or Arminius, by Montanus or Barclay, or the Archbishop of Cambray, is highly probable. But it cannot thence be inferred that I hold "a medley of all their principles—Calvinism, Arminianism, Montanism, Quakerism, Quietism—all thrown together." There might as well have been added Judaism, Mohammedanism, and Paganism. It would have made the period rounder, and been full as easily proved; I mean asserted. For no other proof is yet produced.

31. I pass over the smaller mistakes which occur in the fifteenth and sixteenth paragraphs, together with the prophecy or prognostication concerning the approaching divisions and downfall of the Methodists. What follows to the end, concerning the ground of our hope, is indeed of greater importance. But we have not as yet the strength of the cause; the dissertation promised, is still behind. Therefore, as my work is great, and my time short, I waive that dispute for the present.

Perhaps, when I shall have received further light, I may be convinced that "gospel holiness," as Mr. Tucker believes, "is a necessary qualification, prior to justification." This appears to me now to be directly opposite to the gospel of Christ. But I will endeavor impartially to consider what shall be advanced in defense of it. And may He who knows my simpleness, teach me his way, and give me a right judgment in all things!

Endnotes

1. "Mr. Charles Wesley," the note says, "was not persuaded of the truth of the Moravian faith, til some time after his brother's return from Germany." There is a great mistake in this. I returned not from Germany till Saturday, September 16. My brother was fully persuaded of the truth of the Moravian faith (so called) on Wednesday, May 3, preceding. The note adds, "This justifying faith he received but very lately." This also is a mistake. What he believed to be justifying faith, he received May 21, 1738. (Vol. I. pp. 93, 96.).

2. The next note runs thus: "Mr. Wesley has such a peculiar turn and tendency

towards inconsistencies in his principles, that in his Preface to *Haliburton's Life*, (written February 9, 1738-9, just after his return from Germany) he contradicts all that he has said elsewhere for this sinless perfection; *viz.*, 'But it may be said, the gospel covenant does not promise entire freedom from sin. What do you mean by the word sin—the infection of nature, or those numberless weaknesses and follies, sometimes (improperly) termed sins of infirmity? If you mean only this, you say most true. We shall not put off these but with our bodies. But if you mean, it does not promise entire freedom from sin, in its proper sense, or from committing sin, this is by no means true, unless the Scriptures are false. For thus it is written, *Whosoever is born of God doth not commit sin*, unless he lose the Spirit of adoption, if not finally, yet for a while, as did this child of God: *For his seed remaineth in him, and he cannot sin, because he is born of God.* He cannot sin, so long as he keepeth himself; for then the wicked one toucheth him not.'"

The question is not whether this is right or wrong, but whether it contradicts anything I have said elsewhere. Three times I have spoken expressly on this subject—in a sermon, and in two prefaces. If in any of these I have contradicted what I said before, I will own the former assertion as a mistake.

PART III:
THE PRINCIPLES OF A METHODIST
FARTHER EXPLAINED

Occasioned by the Rev. Mr. Church's second letter to Mr. Wesley
In a second letter to that gentleman

Reverend Sir,

1. AT THE TIME THAT I was reading your former letter, I expected to hear from you again. I was not displeased with the expectation, believing it would give me a fresh opportunity of weighing the sentiments I might have too lightly espoused, and the actions which perhaps I had not enough considered. Viewing things in this light, I cannot but esteem you, not an enemy, but a friend, and one, in some respects, better qualified to do me real service than those whom the world accounts so. They may be hindered by their prejudice in my favour, either from observing what is reprovable, or from using that freedom or plainness of speech which are necessary to convince me of it.

2. It is, at least, as much with a view to learn myself, as to show others (what I think) the truth, that I intend to set down a few reflections on some parts of the tract you have lately published. I say *some* parts, for it is not my design to answer every sentence in this way any more than in the former. Many things I pass over, because I think them true; many more, because I think them not material; and some, because I am determined not to engage in a useless, if not hurtful, controversy.

3. Fear, indeed, is one cause of my declining this; fear, as I said elsewhere,[1] not of my adversary, but of myself. I fear my own spirit, lest "I fall where many mightier have been slain." I never knew one (or but one) man write controversy with what I thought a right spirit. Every disputant seems to think, as every soldier, that he may hurt his opponent as much as he can—oh, no, that he ought to do his worst to him—or he cannot make the best of his own cause. As long as he does not belie, or willfully misrepresent him, he must expose him as much as he is able. It is enough, we suppose, if we do not show heat or passion against our adversary. But not to despise him, or endeavor to make others do so, is quite a work of supreme effort.

4. But ought these things to be so? (I speak on the Christian scheme.) Ought we not to love our neighbor as ourselves? Does a man cease to be our neighbor, because he is of a different opinion, oh, no, and declares himself so to be? Ought we not, for all this, to do to him as we would he

should do to us? But do we ourselves love to be exposed, or set in the worst light? Would we willingly be treated with contempt? If not, why do we treat others thus? And yet, who scruples it? Who does not hit every blot he can, however foreign to the merits of the cause? Who, in controversy, casts the mantle of love over the nakedness of his brother? Who keeps steadily and uniformly to the question, without ever striking at the person? Who shows in every sentence that he loves his brother only less than the truth?

5. I fear neither you nor I have attained to this. I believe brotherly love might have found a better construction than that of unfairness, art, or insincerity, to have put either on my not answering every part of your book (a thing which never once entered my thoughts) or on my not reciting all the words of those parts which I did answer. I cannot yet perceive any blame herein. I still account it fair and innocent to pass over both what I believe is right, and what I believe is not dangerously wrong. Neither can I see any insincerity at all in quoting only that part of any sentence, against which I conceive the objection lies, nor in abridging any part of any treatise to which I reply, whether in the author's or in my own words.

6. If, indeed, it were so abridged as to alter the sense, this would be unfair. If this were intentionally done, it would be crafty and insincere. But I am not conscious of having done this at all, although you speak as if I had done it a thousand times. Yet I cannot undertake now either to transcribe your whole book, or every page or paragraph which I answer. But I must generally abridge before I reply, and that not only to save time (of which I have none to spare) but often to make the argument clearer, which is best understood when couched in few words.

7. You complain also of my mentioning all at once sentences which you placed at a distance from each other. I do so; and I think it quite fair and innocent to lay together what was before scattered abroad.

For instance: You now speak of the conditions of justification, in the eighteenth and following pages; again, from the eighty-ninth to the hundred and second; and yet again, in the hundred and twenty-seventh page. Now, I have not leisure to follow you to and fro. Therefore, what I say on one topic, I set in one place.

A. 1. This said, I come to the letter itself. I begin, as before, with the case of the Moravians, of whom you say, "I collected together the character which you had given of these men; the errors and vices which you had charged upon them and the mischiefs . . . they had done among your followers. And I proved that, in several respects, you had been the occasion of this mischief, and are therefore in some measure, accountable for it. Let us see what answer you give to all this.

"'With regard to the denying degrees in faith, you mentioned that the Moravian Church was cleared from this mistake.' But did you not mention this as one of the tenets of the Moravians? Do you not say that you 'could not agree with Mr. Spangenberg, that no one has any faith so long as he is liable to any doubt or fear?' Do you not represent Mr. Molther, and other Moravians in England, as teaching the same? In short, I have not accused the Moravian Church of anything, but only repeat after you. And if you have accused them when you knew them to be guiltless, you must bear the blame.

"'They use the ordinances of God with reverence and godly fear.' You have accused Mr. Spangenberg and Mr. Molther of teaching that we ought to abstain from them. And the same you say in general of the Moravian brethren, in your letter to them. 'But Mr. Molther was quickly after recalled into Germany.' This might be on other accounts. You do not say it was out of any dislike of his doctrines or proceedings. Nor indeed can you, consistent with your next words: 'The great fault of the Moravian Church seems to lie in not openly disclaiming all he had said, which, in all probability they would have done, had they not leaned to the same opinion.'

"You never knew but one of the Moravian Church affirm that a believer does not grow in holiness.' But who was this? No less a person than Count Zinzendorf, their great Bishop and patron, whose authority is very high, all in all with them, and to whom you think they pay too much regard." (*Second Letter*, page 79.)

2. This is the whole of your reply to this part of my answer. I will now consider it, part by part.

First. "With regard to the denying degrees in faith, you mentioned 'that the Moravian Church was cleared from this mistake.' But did you not mention this as one of the tenets of the Moravians?" No, not of the Moravians in general.

"Do you not say that you 'could not agree with Mr. Spangenberg, that no one has any faith, so long as he is liable to any doubt or fear?'"

I do say so still. But Spangenberg is not the Moravian Church.

"Do you not represent Mr. Molther, and other Moravians in England, as teaching the same?" I do, three or four in all. But neither are these the Moravian Church.

"In short, I have not accused the Moravian Church of anything, but only repeat after you." Indeed you have, in the very case before us. You accuse them of denying degrees in faith. I do not accuse them of this. I openly cleared them from any such charge nearly six years ago.

"If, therefore, you have accused them when you knew them to be guiltless, you must bear the blame." In this case I must entreat you to bear it in my stead, for I have not accused them, the Moravian Church. It is you that have accused them. I have again and again declared they are not guilty.

Secondly. "'They use the ordinances of God with reverence and godly fear.' You have accused Mr. Spangenberg and Mr. Molther of teaching that we ought to abstain from them." That *we*? No. That unbelievers ought. The assertion relates to them only.

"And the same you say in general of the Moravian brethren, in your letter." I say, they hold that unbelievers ought to abstain from them. But yet I know and bear witness, they use them themselves, and that "with reverence and godly fear."

"'Mr. Molther was quickly after recalled to Germany.' This might be on other accounts. You do not say it was out of any dislike of his doctrines or proceedings." I do not say so, because I am not sure. I believe it was out of a dislike for some of his proceedings, if not of his doctrines, too.

"Nor indeed can you, consistent with your next words: 'The great fault of the Moravian Church seems to lie in not openly disclaiming all he had said'" relating to this topic. They did privately disclaim what he had said of degrees in faith, but I think that was not enough. I still believe they would have done more, "had they not leaned themselves to the same opinion," concerning the ordinances.

Thirdly. "You 'never knew but one of the Moravian Church affirm that a believer does not grow in holiness.' But who was this? No less a person than Count Zinzendorf, their great Bishop and patron, whose authority is very high, all in all with them, and to whom you think they pay 'too much regard.'" Do you understand where the stress of the argument lies? I never heard one Moravian affirm this, but the Count alone—and him only once, and that once was in the heat of dispute. Therefore, I inferred it is not a doctrine of the Moravian Church; oh, no, I doubt whether it is the Count's own settled judgment.

3. But I may not dismiss this passage yet. It is now my turn to complain of unfair usage, of the exceeding lame, broken, imperfect manner wherein you cite my words. For instance, your citation runs thus: You "never knew but one of the Moravian Church affirm that a believer does not grow in holiness." My words are these: "I never knew one of the Moravian Church, but that single person, affirm that a believer does not grow in holiness, and perhaps he would not affirm it on reflection." Now, why was the former part of the sentence changed, and the latter quite left out? Had the whole stood in your tract just as it does in mine, it must have appeared I do not here accuse the Moravian Church.

I complain also of your manner of replying to the first article of this very paragraph. You do not cite so much as one line of that answer to which you profess to reply. My words are, "You ought not to accuse the Moravian Church of the first of these" errors, "since in the very page from which you quote those words, 'There is no justifying faith where there ever is any doubt,' that note occurs, (*viz,* Vol. I. p. 328). 'In the preface to the *Second Journal*, the Moravian Church is cleared from this mistake.'" If you had cited these words, could you possibly have added, "I have not accused the Moravian Church of anything, but only repeat after you?"

4. I have now considered one page of your reply, in the manner you seem to require. But surely you cannot expect I should follow you thus, step by step, through a hundred and forty pages! If you should then think it worthwhile to make a second reply, and to follow me in the same manner, we might write indeed, but who would read? I return therefore to what I proposed at first, *viz.*, to touch only on what seems of the most importance, and leave the rest just as it lies.

5. You say, "With regard to subtlety, evasion, and disguise, you now would have it thought that you only found this 'in many of them, not in all, nor in most.'" (Page 80) "You now would have it thought!" Yes, and always, as well as now. For my original complaint was, "I have found this in many of you; that is, much subtlety, much evasion and disguise." (Vol. I. p. 327)

But you add, "Let the reader judge from the following passages, whether you did not charge the Moravians in general with these crimes: 'I had a long conference with those whom I esteem very highly in love, but I could not yet understand them in one point — Christian openness and plainness of speech. They pleaded for such a reservedness and closeness of conversation. Yet I scarcely know what to think, considering they had the practice of the whole Moravian Church on their side.'" True, in pleading for such a reservedness of conversation as I could not in any wise approve of, but not in using much subtlety, much evasion and disguise. This I dare not accuse on the whole Moravian Church.

Those words also—"There is darkness and closeness in all their behavior, and guile in almost all their words"—I spoke, not of all the Moravians, nor of most, but of those who were then in England. I could not speak it of them all, for I never found any guile in Christian David, Michael Linner, and many others.

6. "We are next to see how you get over the objection I made good, in three several particulars, that you have prepared the way for spreading of these tenets. The first you say nothing to here. The second you quote very partially thus: 'By tolerating and commending them.' And why would you not add, 'And being the occasion of so many of them coming over among us?'" Because I was not the occasion. I was indeed the first Englishman that ever was at Hernhuth. But before I was at Hernhuth (I find on later inquiry) the Count himself had been in England.

"You 'still think, that next to some thousands in our own Church, the body of the Moravian Church, however mistaken some of them are, are in general, the best Christians in the world.'" (Page 81.) I do, "of all whom I have seen." You should not omit these words.

"Those dreadful errors and crimes are here softened into mistakes." I term them "errors of judgment and practice."

"I have proved that you have accused the body of such." At present, the proof does not amount to demonstration. There needs to be a little further proof that I accuse any "dreadful crimes" on the body of the Moravians.

I see no manner of inconsistency still, in those accounts of my intercourse with the Moravians, which you suppose irreconcilable with each other. Let anyone read them in the *Journal*, and judge.

7. "You had said, your 'objections then were nearly the same as now.' You now add, 'only with this difference: I was not then assured

that the facts were as I supposed, I did not dare to determine anything.' No! Not when by conversing among them you saw these things? As indeed the facts are of such a nature that you could not but be assured of them, if they were true. Nor do the questions in your Letter really imply any doubt of their truth, but they are so many appeals to their consciences, and equivalent to strong assertions. And if you had not been assured, if you did not dare to determine anything concerning what you saw, your writing bare suspicions to a body of men in such a manner was inexcusable. This excuse, therefore, will not serve you." (Page 83.) I think it will. "I was not then [in September, 1738] assured that the facts were as I supposed." Therefore, "I did not" then "dare to determine anything." Be pleased to add the immediately following words: "But from November 1 [1739] I saw more and more things which I could not reconcile with the Gospel."

If you had not omitted these words, you could have had no color to remark on my saying, "I did not dare to determine anything"

"No! Not when by conversing among them you saw these things?" No, I did not "dare to determine," in September, 1738, from what I saw in November, 1739.

"But the facts are of such a nature, that you could not but be assured of them, if they were true." I cannot think so.

"Is not the Count all in all among you? Do not you magnify your own Church too much? Do you not use dishonesty and disguise in many cases?" These facts are by no means of such a nature, as that whoever converses (even intimately) among the Moravians cannot help but be assured of them.

"Nor do the questions in your Letter really imply any doubt of their truth." No! Are not my very words prefixed to those questions? "Of some other things I stand in doubt. And I wish that, in order to remove those doubts, you would plainly answer, whether the facts are as I suppose."

"But" these questions "are so many appeals to their consciences." True.

"And equivalent to strong assertions." Utterly false.

"If you had not been assured, if you did not dare to determine anything concerning what you saw" (fifteen months after) "your writing bare suspicions to a body of men in such a manner was inexcusable." They were strong presumptions then, which yet I did not write to a body of men, whom I so highly esteemed; no, not even in the tenderest manner, till I was assured they were not groundless.

8. "In a note at the bottom of page 8, you observe, 'The Band Society in London began May 1, some time before I set out for Germany.' Would you insinuate here, that you did not set it up in imitation of the Moravians?" Sir, I will tell you the naked truth. You had remarked thus: "You took the trouble of a journey to Germany to them. You were so much in love with their methods that at your return you set up their Bands among your disciples." (Page 17.) This was an entire mistake. That society was set up, not only before I returned, but before I set out. I designed that note to inform you without telling your mistake to all the world.

"I imagined, that, supposing your account of the Moravians were true, it would be impossible for any serious Christian to doubt of their being very wicked people." I know many serious Christians who suppose it is true, and yet believe they are in general, good men. "A much worse character, take the whole body together, cannot be given of a body of men." Let us try: "Here is a body of men who have not one either of justice, mercy, or truth among them, they are lost to all sense of right and wrong. They have neither sobriety, temperance, nor chastity. They are, in general, liars, drunkards, gluttons, thieves, adulterers, murderers." I cannot help but think that this is a much worse character than that of the Moravians, take it how you will. "Let the reader judge how far you are now able to defend them." Just as far as I did at first. Still I dare not condemn what is good among them, and I will not excuse what is evil.

9. "'The Moravians excel in sweetness of behavior.' What, though they use dishonesty and disguise?" Yes.

"'Where is their multitude of errors?' In your own *Journal*. I have taken the pains to place them in one view in my *Remarks,* the justness of which, with all your art, you cannot disprove." You have taken the pains to transcribe many words. All of them together amount to this: that they, generally, hold universal salvation, and are partly Antinomians (in opinion) partly Quietists. The justness of some of your remarks, if I mistake not, has been pretty fully disproved. As to what you speak of my art, subtlety, and so on, in this and many other places, I look upon it as neither better nor worse than a civil way of calling names.

"'To this multitude of crimes I am also an utter stranger.' Then you have charged them wrongfully. What do you account dishonesty?" etc. (*Second Letter*, p. 84.) I account dishonesty, despising self-denial even in the smallest points, and teaching that those who have not the assurance of faith may not use the ordinances of God, the Lord's Supper in particular (this is the real, unaggravated charge) to be faults which cannot be excused. But I do not account them all together "a multitude of crimes." I conceive this is a vehement exaggeration.

"The honor of religion," said you, "and virtue trampled upon." I answered, "By whom? Not by the Moravians." You reply, "And yet you have accused some of these as discrediting all the means of grace." No. What I accused them of was teaching that an unbeliever (in their sense) ought to abstain from them.

"'Neither did I know, or think, or say, they were desperately wicked people.' Your *Journal* is before the world, to whom I appeal whether this has not so represented them." But how do you here represent your remark, and my answer? My paragraph runs thus:

"You go on, 'How could you so long, and so intimately, converse with such desperately wicked people as the Moravians, according to your own account, were known by you to be? 'Oh Sir, what another assertion is this!' The Moravians, according to your own account, were known by you to be desperately wicked people, while you intimately conversed with them! 'Utterly false and injurious! I never gave any such account. I conversed with them intimately both at Savannah and Hernhuth. But neither then nor at any other time did I know, or think, or say, they were desperately wicked people. I think and say just the reverse, *viz.*, that though I soon 'found among them a few things which I could not approve, yet I believe they are, in general, some of the best Christians in the world.' After this, are you the person who complains of me for imperfect and partial quotations?" (Page 10.)

I added, "You surprise me yet more in going on thus: 'In God's name, Sir, is the contempt of almost the whole of our duty, of every Christian ordinance, to be so very gently touched?' Sir, this is not the case. This charge no more belongs to the Moravians than that of murder." (Page 11.)

You reply, "Mr. Spangenberg and Mr. Molther are accused by name. If falsely, I am sorry both for them and you." *Accused?* True. But of what — of the contempt of every Christian ordinance, of almost the whole of our duty? By no means. The plain case is, I accuse them of one thing, *viz.*, teaching that an unbeliever should abstain from the ordinances. You accuse them of another: condemning every Christian ordinance, and almost the whole of our duty, and this you would father upon me. I desire to be excused.

10. As to what I said in my letter to the Moravian Church—"You can hinder this if you will. Therefore, if you do not prevent their speaking thus, you do, in effect, speak thus yourselves" — it may be observed, (1.) That this letter is dated August 8, 1741. (2.) That from that time the Moravian Church did in great measure prevent any of their members speaking thus.

You proceed: "You distinguish between the English brethren and the Moravians. These English brethren, I presume, were your followers. Afterwards you represent them as perverted by the Moravians: 'Before they had spoke these wicked things,' you say, 'they had joined these men, and acted under their direction.' If they did not learn them from these new teachers, from whom did they learn them? Not, surely, from yourself, or any other Methodists. You cannot, therefore, bring off the Moravians without condemning your own people. Here, therefore, you have certainly overshot yourself." (Page 85.) Perhaps not. "These English brethren were, I presume, your followers." No, this is your first mistake. I was but a single, private member of that society. "Afterwards you represent them as perverted by the Moravians." I do, but not yet connected with them.

"Before they spoke these wicked things, they had joined these men, and acted under their direction." This is another mistake. They did not join these men, nor act by their direction, till long after. "If they did not learn them from these new teachers, from whom did they learn them? You cannot bring off the Moravians without condemning your own people." They learned them from Mr. Molther chiefly, whom I am not at all concerned to bring off. Now let all men judge which of us two has overshot himself.

11. "In answer to my objections against the inconsistent accounts you have given of the Moravians, you say, 'They are, I believe, the most self-inconsistent people under the sun.' Would not one imagine that you here speak of the same persons, or of the whole body of them in

general?" I do, thus far: I ascribe the good to the body of them in general, the evil to part only of that body, to some of those same persons.

"Your method of getting over the contradictions I had charged upon you is much the same—to distinguish either between the Moravians and the English brethren, though these had been their disciples [this has been abundantly answered] or between some of the Moravians and others." (Page 86.) I think it is a very good method, for propositions are not contradictory unless they both speak of the same persons.

However, since you persist to affirm that I am guilty of the contradictions you charged upon me (page 87) I think there cannot be a sufficient reply without reciting the several instances.

12. First. "You commend them (the Moravians) for loving one another and yet accuse them of biting and devouring one another." I answered, "*Them!* Whom? Not the Moravians, but the English brethren of Fetter Lane, before their union with the Moravians. Here, then, is no shadow of contradiction, for the two sentences do not relate to the same persons."

You reply, "Would you then have us to think that so much anger and contradiction reigned among your Methodists?" I would have you think this is nothing to the purpose. Prove the contradiction, and you speak to the point. "It is plain they had before this been perverted by the Moravians, and that they were unwilling to be taught by any others." *They*, that is, nearly half of the society. But here is no proof of the contradiction still.

(2.) "You say, 'They had nearly destroyed brotherly love from among us, partly by cautions against natural love, partly by occasioning almost continual disputes.'" So they had, but we had then no connection with them. Neither, therefore, does this contradict their loving one another.

You reply, "As if they can truly love each other, who teach you not to do it, and stir up divisions and disturbances among you." You should say, if you would repeat after me, "Who caution you against natural love, and occasion many disputes among you." Well, allowing they do this (which is utterly wrong) yet where is the contradiction? Yet they may love one another.

(3.) "You praise them for using no recreation, but such as are appropriate for saints, and yet say [I recite the whole sentence] 'I have heard some of you affirm that Christian salvation implies liberty to conform to the world, by joining in worldly recreations in order to do good.'" Both these are true. The Moravians, in general, use no recreations but such as are appropriate for saints. And yet I have heard some of them affirm, in contradiction to their own practice, that "one then mentioned did well when he joined in playing tennis in order to do good." To this you make no reply. Silence then consents, that there is no contradiction here.

(4.) "You 'praise them for not regarding outward adorning.'" So I do, the bulk of the congregation. "And yet you say [I again recite the whole sentence] 'I have heard some of you affirm that Christian salvation implies liberty to conform to the world, by putting on gold and costly apparel.'" I have said so; and I blame them the more, because "they are condemned by the general practice of their own Church." To this also you reply not. So I must count this the fourth contradiction which you have charged upon me, but have not proved.

(5.) "You call their discipline, in most respects, truly excellent. I could wish you had more fully explained yourself. 'I have, in the *Second Journal*,' Vol. I. pp. 115-147. It is no sign of good discipline to permit such abominations; that is, error in opinion and dishonesty in practice. 'True. It is not, nor is it any demonstration against it. There may be good discipline even in a college of Jesuits. Another fault is too great a deference to the Count. And yet, in most respects, their discipline is truly excellent.'"

You reply, "Such excellent discipline, for all that I know, they may have [that is, as the Jesuits] but I cannot agree that this is scarcely inferior to that of the Apostolic Age." It may be, for anything you advance to the contrary. "Here I cited some words of yours, condemning their subordination (page 88) which you prudently take no notice of." Yes, I had just before taken notice of their too great deference to the Count. But the contradiction! Where is the contradiction?

(6.) "You mention it as a good effect of their discipline, that 'everyone knows and keeps his proper rank.' Soon after, as though it were designed to refute yourself, you say, 'Our brethren have neither wisdom enough to guide, nor prudence enough to let it alone.'" I answered, "Pardon me, Sir, I have no design either to refute or contradict myself in these words. The former sentence is spoken of the Moravian brethren. The latter, is spoken of the English brethren of Fetter Lane, not then united with the Moravians, neither acting by their direction." To this likewise you do not reply. Here is then a sixth contradiction, alleged against me, but not proved.

13. However, you add, "Had you shown me mistaken in any point

you have attempted to reply to, still you confess errors and wickedness enough among the Moravians to render your account of them very inconsistent. But you have not succeeded in any one answer. You have not shown that I have, in any one instance, misquoted you, or misunderstood the character you had given of them, or argued falsely from what you had said of them. Truly, Sir, all you have done has been picking at a few particulars, but the argument I was urging all this while you quite forgot."

Sir, if it be so, you do me too much honor in setting pen to paper again. But is it so? Have I all this while quite forgotten the argument you were urging? I hope not. I seem to remember you were urging some argument to prove, that I "fall not only into inconsistencies, but direct contradictions;" (*Remarks*, p. 21) and that I showed you mistaken, not only in *one*, but in *every* point which you advanced as such. I did not confess any such errors or wickedness of the Moravians as rendered my account of them self-inconsistent. I "succeeded" in more than "one answer" to the objections you had urged against it. I showed you had "misquoted or misunderstood the character I had given of them," or "argued falsely from it," not properly "in one instance," but from the beginning to the end.

Yet this I think it is my responsibility to say, that whereever I have contributed, directly or indirectly, to the spreading of anything evil, which is or has been among the Moravians, I am sorry for it, and hereby ask pardon both of God and all the world.

B. 1. I think it appears, by what you have yourself observed, that, on the Second topic, Justification by Faith, I allow, in the beginning of the *Farther Appeal*, almost as much as you contend for.

I would like your permission to cite part of that passage again, that we may come as near each other as possible. I would just add a few words on each topic, which I hope may remove more difficulties out of the way:

"That justification, whereof our Articles and Homilies speak, means present pardon, and acceptance with God, who therein 'declares his righteousness,' or mercy, 'by' or 'for the remission of sins that are past.'"

I say, *past*, for I cannot find anything in the Bible of the remission of sins, past, present, and to come.

"I believe the condition of this is faith. I mean not only that without faith we cannot be justified, but also that as soon as anyone has true faith, in that moment he is justified."

You take the word *condition* in the former sense only, as that without which we cannot be justified. In this sense of the word, I think we may allow, that there are several conditions of justification.

"Good works follow this faith, but cannot go before it. Much less can sanctification, which implies a continued course of good works, springing from holiness of heart." Yet such a course is, without doubt, absolutely necessary to our continuance in a state of justification.

"It is allowed that repentance and 'fruits proper for repentance' go before faith. Repentance absolutely must go before faith; fruits proper for it, if there is opportunity. By repentance I mean conviction of sin, producing real desires and sincere resolutions of amendment. By 'fruits proper for repentance,' I mean forgiving our brother, ceasing from evil, doing good, using the ordinances of God, and in general obeying him according to the measure of grace which we have received. But these I cannot as yet term good works, because they do not spring from faith and the love of God," although the same works are then good, when they are performed by "those who have believed."

"Faith, in general, is a divine, supernatural $ελεγχος$ (evidence or conviction) of things not seen, not discoverable by our bodily senses, as being either past, future, or spiritual. Justifying faith implies not only a divine $ελεγχος$, that God was in Christ, reconciling the world to himself, but a sure trust and confidence that Christ died for my sins, that he loved me, and gave himself for me. The moment a penitent sinner thus believes, God pardons and absolves him."

I say, *a penitent sinner*; because justifying faith cannot exist without previous repentance.

"Yet, although both repentance and the fruits thereof are in some sense necessary before justification, neither the one nor the other is necessary in the same sense, or in the same degree, with faith. Not in the same degree, for in whatever moment a man believes (in the Christian sense of the word) he is justified. But it is not so at whatever moment he repents, or brings forth any, or all, of the fruits of repentance. Consequently, none of these are necessary to justification in the same degree with faith.

"Nor in the same sense. For none of these has so direct, immediate a relation to justification as faith. This is closely necessary to it. Repentance is remote, as it is necessary to faith. [So the error of the press is to be corrected.] And the fruits of repentance are still more remote, as they are necessary to the increase or continuance of repentance. Even in this sense, they are only necessary on supposition, if there is time and opportunity for them. For in many instances there is not, but God cuts short his work, and faith occurs before the fruits of repentance."

2. Thus far I believe we are nearly agreed. But on those words—"Far other qualifications are required in order to our standing before God in glory, than were required in order to his giving us faith and pardon. In order to this, nothing is indispensably required, but repentance, or conviction of sin. But in order to the other, it is indispensably required, that we be fully cleansed from all sin"—you remark, "Here, I understand, are two great mistakes: (1.) You make too little necessary before pardon. (2.) Too much afterward. You confine repentance within too narrow limits, and extend holiness beyond its just bounds.

"First. By repentance you mean only conviction of sin, but this is a very partial account of it. Every child that has learned his Catechism can tell that forsaking of sin is included in it. He must be living in obedience to God's will, when there is opportunity; and even when there is not, there must be a sincere desire and purpose to do so, and a faith in God's mercies through Christ Jesus." (Page 92.)

I had said, "In order to God's giving us faith and pardon, nothing is indispensably required but repentance," that is, "conviction of sin, producing real desires and sincere resolutions of amendment." But you "understand that I am here in a great mistake," that I give a "very partial account of repentance," that I ought to "include therein a sincere desire and purpose" to obey God. I do. I have said so expressly: and "living in obedience to God's will, when there is opportunity." Very well, but here I speak of what is indispensably required, that is, whether there is opportunity of actual obedience or not. "And a faith in God's mercies through Christ Jesus." A very great mistake indeed, my not including faith in that repentance which I say is indispensably required in order to faith!

"Secondly. You make sinless perfection necessary after justification, in order to make us fit for glory." And who does not? Indeed men do not agree in the time. Some believe it is attained before death; some, in the article of death; some, in an after-state, in the Mystic or the Popish purgatory. But all writers, whom I have ever seen till now (the Romish themselves not excepted) agree that we must be "fully cleansed from all sin" before we can enter into glory.

3. After what has already been allowed, I cannot think it needful to dispute farther on the topic of justification. Rather suffer me to close this part of our debate, by transcribing what I assent to, from that clear recounting of your thoughts which you have given in pages 4, and 46:

(1.) "Justification is the act of God, pardoning our sins, and receiving us again to his favour. This was free in him, because it is undeserved by us; undeserved, because we had transgressed his law, and could not, nor even can now perfectly fulfill it.

(2.) "We cannot, therefore, be justified by our works. This would be, to be justified by some merit of our own. Much less can we be justified by an external show of religion or by any superstitious observances.

(3.) "The life and death of our Lord is the sole meritorious cause of this mercy, which must be firmly believed and trusted in by us. Our faith therefore in him, though not more meritorious than any other of our actions, yet has a nearer relation to the promises of pardon through him, and is the means and instrument by which we embrace and receive them.

(4.) "True faith must be lively and productive of good works, which are its proper fruits, the traits by which it is known.

(5.) "Works really good are such as are commanded by God (springing from faith) done by the aid of his Holy Spirit with good intentions, and to good ends. These may be considered as internal or external.

(6.) "The inward ones—such as hope, trust, fear, and love of God and our neighbor (which may be more properly termed *good dispositions*, and [are branches of] sanctification)—must always be joined with faith, and consequently be conditions present in justification, though they are not the means or instruments of receiving it.

(7.) "The outward, [which are more properly termed good works) though there be no immediate opportunity of practicing them, and therefore a sincere desire and resolution to perform them is sufficient for the present. Yet they must follow after as soon as occasion offers, and will then be necessary conditions of preserving our justification.

(8.) "There is a justification conveyed to us in our baptism, or properly, this state is then begun. But should we fall into sins we cannot regain it without true faith and repentance, which implies (as its fruits) a forsaking of our sins, and correction of our whole life."

I have only one circumstance farther to add, namely that I am not newly convinced of these things. This is the doctrine which I have continually taught for eight or nine years past. I only abstained from the word *condition* perhaps more scrupulously than was needful.

4. With regard to the consequences of my teaching this doctrine, I desire any who will not count it lost labor, to consult with his own eyes, seriously and in the fear of God, the *Third* and *Fourth Journals*. If he pleases, he may further read over and compare, from the 395th to the 397th page of my answer, with your reply, from the one hundred and first inclusive, to the one hundred and fourth page.

Among the consequences you reckoned (in your *Remarks*) besides, "introducing predestination, confusion, presumption, and despair, many very shocking instances of all which [your words are] you give us among your followers." (Pages 52, 55.) I answered, "You should have specified a few of those instances, at least the pages where they occur. (Suppose, only three of each sort, out of any or all the four *Journals*.) Till this is done, I can look upon this assertion as no other than a flourish of your pen."

Upon this you exclaim, (Page 111) "I must beg the reader to observe your method of citing my words. Many instances of omissions he has had already. But here is such a one, as I believe few controversies can parallel. Would not anyone imagine from the view of these words [Predestination, confusion, presumption, and despair] that they occurred all together in page fifty-two of my *Remarks*, and that I observed nothing farther concerning this point? Could it be thought that anything intervened between the page referred to, and the last sentence? And yet so it is, that nearly three pages intervene!" Ha! Do *nearly three pages intervene!* Prodigious indeed? "And this is called an answer!" So it is, for want of a better.

"Your business was to show, that the Calvinistical notions have not prevailed among the Methodists, or that they were not consequences of unconditional justification." No, Sir, it was not my business to show this. It was not my business to prove the negative, but yours to prove the affirmative. Mr. Whitefield is himself a Calvinist. Such therefore doubtless are many of his followers. But Calvinism has not prevailed at all among any other of the Methodists (so called) nor is it to this day any consequence of unconditional justification in the manner wherein I preach it.

5. You next "take the pains to lay before the reader an instance or two of confusion," etc. The first I read thus:

"While we were at the room Mrs. J., sitting at home, took the Bible to read, but on a sudden threw it away, saying, 'I am good enough. I will never read or pray more.' She was in the same mind when I came, often repeating, 'I used to think I was full of sin, and that I sinned in everything I did, but now I know better. I am a good Christian. I never did any harm in my life. I do not desire to be any better than I am.' She spoke many things to the same effect, plainly showing that the spirit of pride and of lies had the full dominion over her.

"I asked, 'Do you desire to be healed?'

"She said, 'I am whole.'

"'But do you desire to be saved?'

"She replied, 'I am saved. I am not sick. I am happy.'

"This is one of the fruits of the present salvation and sinless perfection taught by you among the weak and ignorant." (Page 11.)

I should wonder if the scarecrow of sinless perfection was not brought in some way or other, but to the point. You here repeat a relation as from me, and that "in confirmation," you say, "of your own veracity," and yet leave out both the beginning of that narration, part of the middle, and the end of it.

I begin thus: "Sun. 11—I met with a surprising instance of the power of the devil." (Vol. I. p. 295.) These words, of all others, should not have been left out, being a key to all that follows. In the middle of the narration, immediately after the words, "I am happy," I add, "Yet it was easy to discern she was in the most violent agony both of body and mind; sweating exceedingly, despite the severe frost, and not continuing in the same posture a moment:"—This is plain proof that this was no instance of presumption, nor a natural fruit of any teaching whatever.

It ends thus: "About a quarter before six the next morning, after lying quiet a while, she broke out, 'Peace to you [her husband]; peace to this house. The peace of God is come to my soul. *I know that my Redeemer liveth.*' And for several days her mouth was filled with his praise, and her talk was wholly of his wondrous works."

Had not these words been left out, neither could this have passed for an instance of despair. Though still I do not know but it might have stood for an instance of confusion, etc.

I must not forget that this was cited at first as a proof of my enthusiasm [fanaticism] as an instance of a private revelation, "which," you say, I "seem to pay great credit to—representing the conjectures of a woman whose brain appears to have been too much heated, as if they had been owing to a particular and miraculous spirit of prophecy." (*Remarks*, p. 64.)

I answered, "Talk on, Sir, as you please on this enthusiasm; on the credit I paid to this private revelation; and my representing the conjectures of this brain-sick woman as owing to a miraculous power of the Spirit of prophecy. When you have done, I will desire you to read the passage once more, where you will find my express words are, introducing this account: 'Sun. 11—I met with a surprising instance of the power of the devil.' Such was the 'credit' I paid to this revelation! All I ascribe to the Spirit of God is the enabling her to strive against the power of the devil, and at length restoring peace to her soul." (*Answer*, page 408.)

I was in hopes you had done with this example, but I am disappointed, for in your Second Letter I read thus:

"The instances of enthusiasm and presumption which your last *Journal* had furnished me remain now to be reviewed. The first was of a private revelation, which you appeared to pay great credit to. You had represented everything the woman had spoken in her agony as coming to pass." (Page 130.) But I had not represented anything she spoke then, whether it came to pass or not, as coming from the Spirit of God but from the devil.

You say, "When I read this first I was amazed, and impatient to look again into your *Journal*. I had no sooner done this but I was still more astonished, for you have very grievously misrepresented the case." If I have, then I will bear the blame. If not, it will light on your head.

"It is not *this* account which you had thus introduced, but another, and a very different one, of what happened a day or two before. Sunday, you mention her as being guilty of gross presumption, which you attribute to the power of the devil. But on Monday and Tuesday the opposite revelations happened, which you relate without the least mark of embarrassment or blame." (*Ibid.* p. 131.)

I am grieved that you constrain me to say any more. In the sixty-sixth and sixty-seventh pages of the last *Journal*[2] I gave account of Mrs. Jones, which I term "a surprising instance of the power of the devil." It includes the occurrences of three days. This you brought as a proof of my enthusiasm. I answer,

"The very words that introduce this account," prove it is no instance of enthusiasm. I mean by *this account* (as I suppose is plain to every reader) the following account of Mrs. Jones. You reply, "It is not this account, which you had thus introduced, but another, and a very different one, of what happened a day or two before." Sir, it is the whole account of Mrs. Jones which I thus introduce, and not another, not a very different one. I attribute the agony which she (Mrs. Jones) was in, and most of the words which she spoke on Sunday, Monday, and Tuesday, not to the Spirit of God, but to the power of the devil.

6. The next instance which you relate as an instance of despair is that of a young woman of Kingswood. Which you break off with, "Take me away, etc." (Page 112.) But why did you not decipher that "etc."? Why did you not add the rest of the paragraph? Because it would have spoiled your whole argument. It would have shown what the end of the Lord was in permitting that severe visitation. The words are, "We interrupted her by calling again upon God, on which she sunk down as before (as one asleep) and another young woman began to roar as loudly as she had done. My brother now came in, it being about nine o'clock. We continued in prayer till past eleven, when God in a moment spoke peace into the soul, first of the first tormented, and then of the other. And they both joined in singing praises to Him who had stilled the enemy and the avenger." (Vol. I. p. 235.)

7. I am sorry to find you still affirm that, with regard to the Lord's supper also, I "advance many unwise, false, and dangerous things. Such as, (1.) that 'a man ought to communicate [take Communion] without a sure trust in God's mercy through Christ.'" (Page 117.) You mark these as my words, but I know them not.

(2.) "That there is no previous preparation indispensably necessary, but a desire to receive whatever God pleases to give." But I include abundantly more in that desire than you seem to grasp, even a willingness to know and do the whole will of God.

(3.) "That no fitness is required at the time of communicating [I recite the whole sentence] but a sense of our state, of our utter sinfulness and helplessness! Everyone who knows he is fit for hell, being just fit to come to Christ, in this, as well as in all other ways of his appointment." But neither can this sense of our utter sinfulness and helplessness exist, without earnest desires of universal holiness.

"There was another passage," you say, "which you chose to omit." (Page 118.) Which this was, I do not understand, nor do I perceive any one of these dreadful positions (as you style them) to be contrary to the Word of God.

8. You will likewise, at all hazards, stand your ground, as to the charge of stoical insensibility. I answered before, "How do you support the charge? Why, thus: 'You say, *The servants of God suffer nothing.*' Can you possibly misunderstand these words, if you read those that immediately follow? 'His body was nearly torn apart with pain, but God made all his bed in his sickness. He was continually giving thanks to God and making his boast of his praise.'" (Page 405.)

You reply, "If you meant no more than that a man under the sharpest pains may be thankful to God, why did you call this a strange truth?" (Page 118.) Because I think it is so. I think it exceeding strange, that one in such a degree of pain should be continually giving thanks to God. Not that I suppose him "insensible of his torments." "His body," I say, "was nearly torn apart with pain." But the love of God so abundantly overbalanced all pain, that it was as nothing to him.

"The next instance is as follows: One told you, 'Sir, I thought last week there could be no such rest as you describe, none in this world wherein we should be so free as not to desire ease in pain. But God has taught me better. For on Friday and Saturday, when I was in the strongest pain, I never once had one moment's desire of ease.'" Add, "But only that the will of God might be done."

Neither has this any resemblance of "stoical insensibility." I never supposed that this person did not feel pain (nor indeed that there is any state on earth in which we shall not feel it) but that her soul was filled with the love of God, and thankfully resigned to his will.

"Another instance is taken from one of your hymns, where are these lines: (Page 119.)

> *Doom, if thou canst, to endless pains,*
> *And drive me from thy face:'"*

(Add,

> *"But if thy stronger love constrains,*
> *Let me be saved by grace."*)

"This I thought the height of insensibility, extravagance, and presumption. You see nothing of these in it. And yet you explain yourself thus: 'If you can deny yourself, if you can forget to be gracious, if you can cease to be truth and love.' All of which, in my opinion, is fixing the accusation most strongly upon you, for the supposition that Christ *can* do these things." Are you in earnest, Sir? Are you really so ignorant that expressions of this kind do not suppose he *can*, but quite the reverse — that they are one of the strongest forms of pleading, of calling upon God to show mercy, by all his grace, and truth, and love? So far is this also from proving the charge of "stoical insensibility."

C. 1. I come now to consider the point of Church communion, of which you have spoken in the beginning of your *Treatise*. In the introduction, you say, "We teach no other doctrine than has always been taught in our Church. Our beliefs concerning justification are reconcilable to our Articles, Homilies, and Service. This I understand several of the Methodists have been convinced of, and have therefore left our communion entirely. You give us more instances than one of this in your last *Journal*." (Page 2.) No, not one, nor did I ever yet know one man who "therefore left the communion of the Church" because he was convinced that her Articles, Homilies, or Liturgy opposed his beliefs concerning justification. Poor Mr. St— and Mr. Simpson were induced to leave it by reasons of quite another kind.

You add, "We cannot wonder that some Methodists have withdrawn from her, while they have been used to hear doctrines which they must have understood have no place in her Articles and Service." So far from it that all I know of them are deeply convinced, the "doctrines they have been used to hear" daily are no other than the genuine doctrines of the Church, as expressed both in her Articles and Service.

2. But our present question turns not on doctrine but discipline. "My first business," you say, "is to consider some very lax notions of Church communion which I find in your last *Journal*, Vol. I. p. 262. You say, 'Our Twentieth Article defines a true Church, a congregation of faithful people, in which the true Word of God is preached, and the sacraments duly administered.'" (Page 3.) The use I would willingly make of this

definition (which observe, is not mine, be it good or bad) is to stop the boasting of ungodly men, by cutting off their pretense to call themselves members of the Church. But you think they may call themselves so still. Then let them. I will not contend about it.

But you cannot infer from hence, that my notions of Church communion are either lax or otherwise. The definition which I occasionally cite shows nothing of my beliefs on that topic. For anything which occurs in this page, they may be strict or loose, right or wrong.

You add, "It will be requisite, in order to approve yourself a Minister of our Church, that you follow her rules and orders; that you constantly conform to the method of worship she has prescribed, and study to promote her peace." (Page 5.) All this is good and fit to be done. But it properly belongs to the following question: —

"What led you into such very loose notions of Church communion, I imagine, might be your being conscious to yourself that, according to the strict, just account of the Church of England, you could not with any grace maintain your pretensions to belong still to her." Sir, I have never told you yet what my notions of Church communion are. They may be wrong or they may be right, for all you know. Therefore, when you are first supposing that I have told you my notions, and then assigning the reasons of them, what can be said but that you imagine the whole matter?

3. How far I have acted agreeably to the rules and orders of our Church is a further question. You think I have acted contrary to them, First, by using extemporary [spontaneous, unwritten] prayer in public. "The Church," you say, "has strongly declared her mind on this point, by appointing her excellent Liturgy which you have solemnly promised to use, and no other." I know not when or where. "And whoever does not worship God in the manner she prescribes must be supposed to slight and condemn her offices and rules, and therefore can be no more worthy to be called her Minister." (*Ibid.* p. 7.)

I do not "slight or condemn the offices" of the Church. I esteem them very highly. Yet I do not at all times worship God, even in public, in the very terms of those offices. Nor yet do I knowingly "slight or condemn her rules." It is not clear to my understanding, that she has any rule which forbids using extemporary prayer, let us suppose, between the Morning and Evening Service. And if I am "not worthy to be called her Minister" (which I dare by no means affirm myself to be) yet her Minister I am, and must always be, unless I should be judicially deposed from my ministry.

Your Second argument is this: "If you suppose the Scripture commands you to use extemporary prayer, then you must suppose our Liturgy to be inconsistent with Scripture, and, consequently, unlawful to be used." That does not follow, unless I supposed the Scripture to command us, to use extemporary prayer and no other. Then it would follow that a form of prayer was inconsistent with Scripture. But this I never did suppose.

Your Third argument is to this effect: "You act contrary to the rule of the Church. Allow she is in the wrong, yet, while you break her rule, how do you act as her minister?" It ought to be expressed, "How are you her minister?" for the conclusion to be proved is, that I am not her minister.

I answer, (1.) I am not convinced, as I observed before, that I do hereby break her rule. (2.) If I did, yet should I not cease to be her minister unless I were formally deprived. (3.) I now actually do continue in her communion and hope that I always shall.

4. You object further, that I "disobey the governors of the Church." I answer, I both do and will obey them in all things, where I do not understand there is some particular law of God to the contrary. "Here," you say, "you confess that in some things you do not, and cannot obey your governors." (Page 8.) Did I *confess this*? Then I spoke rashly and foolishly, for I granted more than I can make good. I do certainly understand that the law of God requires me both to preach and, sometimes, to pray *extempore*. Yet I do not know that I disobey the governors of the Church herein, for I do not know that they have forbidden me to do either.

But your "behavior and method of teaching is irregular. Have you any warrant from Scripture for preaching" up and down thus? I think I have. I think God has called me to this work "by the laying on of the hands of the Presbytery," which directs me how to obey that general command, "While we have time, let us do good to all men."

"But we ought to do this agreeably to our respective situations, and not break in upon each other's provinces. Every private man may take upon himself the office of a Magistrate and quote this text as justly as you have done." (Page 9.) No, the private man is not called to the office of a Magistrate, but I am to the office of a Preacher. "You were, indeed, authorized to preach the gospel, but it was in the congregation to which you should be lawfully appointed. You have many years preached in places where you were not lawfully appointed, oh no, which were entrusted to others, who neither needed nor desired your assistance."

Many of them needed it enough, whether they desired it or not. But I shall not now debate that point. I rather follow you to the First Part of the *Farther Appeal*, where this objection is considered.

5. "Our Church," it was said, "has provided against this preaching up and down in the ordination of a Priest, by expressly limiting the exercise of the powers then conferred upon him to the congregation where he shall be lawfully appointed to."

I answered, (1.) "Your argument proves too much. If it be allowed just as you propose it, it proves that no Priest has authority either to preach or administer the sacrament in any other than his own congregation." (*Farther Appeal*, p. 117.)

You reply, "Is there no difference between a thing's being done occasionally, and its being done for years together?" Yes, a great one, and more inconveniences may arise from the latter than from the former. But this is all wide. It does not touch the point. Still, if our Church does expressly limit the exercise of the sacerdotal powers to that congregation to which each Priest shall be appointed, this precludes him from exercising those powers at all in any other than that congregation.

I answered, (2.) "Had the powers conferred been so limited when I was ordained Priest, my ordination would have signified just nothing. I was not appointed to any congregation at all but was ordained as a member of that 'College of Divines' [so our Statutes express it] founded to overturn all heresies, and defend the catholic faith."

You reply, "I presume it was expected you should either continue at your College, or enter upon some regular ministry." Perhaps so, but I must still insist that if my sacerdotal powers had been then expressly limited to that congregation whereunto I should be appointed, my ordination would have signified nothing. I mean I could never, in virtue of that ordination, have exercised those powers at all. I never was appointed to any single congregation, at least not till I went to Georgia.

I answered, (3.) "For many years after I was ordained Priest, this limitation was never heard of. I heard not one syllable of it by way of objection to my preaching up and down in Oxford or London, or the parts adjacent; in Gloucestershire or Worcestershire; in Lancashire, Yorkshire) or Lincolnshire. Nor did the strictest disciplinarian hesitate to allow me to exercise those powers wherever I came."

You reply, "There is great difference between preaching occasionally, with the permission of the incumbents, and doing it constantly without their permission." I grant there is, and there are objections to the latter which do not reach the former case. But they do not belong to this topic. They do not in the least affect this consequence, "If every Priest, when ordained, is expressly limited, touching the exercise of the power then received, to that congregation to which he shall be appointed, then is he precluded by this express limitation from preaching, with or without the incumbent's agreement, in any other congregation whatever."

I answered, (4.) "Is it not, in fact, universally allowed that every Priest, as such, has a power in virtue of his ordination to preach in any congregation, where the Curate desires his assistance?"

You reply to this by what you judge a parallel case, but it does not touch the restriction in question. Either this does, or does not, expressly limit the exercise of the powers conferred upon a Priest in his ordination to that congregation to which he shall be appointed. If it does not, I am not condemned by this, however faulty I may be on a thousand other accounts. If it does, then is every Priest condemned whoever preaches out of the congregation to which he is appointed.

Your parallel case is this: "Because a man does not offend against the law of the land, when I prevail upon him to teach my children," therefore "he is empowered to seize" (read, he does not offend against the law of the land in seizing) "an apartment in my house, and against my will and permission to continue there, and to direct and dictate to my family!" (Page 11.)

An exact parallel indeed! When, therefore, I came to live in St. Luke's parish, was it just the same thing as if I had seized an apartment in Dr. Buckley's house? And was the continuing therein against his will and permission (supposing it were so) precisely the same, as if I had continued in his house, whether he would agree or not? Is the one exactly the same offense against the law of the land as the other?

Once more: Is the warning of sinners in Moorfields to flee from the wrath to come, the very same with directing the Doctor's family under his own roof? I should not have answered this, but that I was afraid you would conclude it was unanswerable.

I answered the former objector, (5.) "Before those words which you suppose to imply such a restraint, were those spoken without any restraint or limitation at all, which I understand to convey an indelible character, 'Receive the Holy Ghost, for the office and work of a Priest in the Church of God, now committed unto you by the laying on of our hands.'" You reply, "The question is not, whether you are in orders or not." (*Ibid.* p. 12.) I am glad to hear it. I really thought it was. "But whether you have acted suitably to the directions or rules of the Church of England." Not suitably to that rule, if it were strictly to be interpreted, of preaching only in a single congregation. I have given my reasons why I think it cannot be so interpreted, and those reasons I do not see that you have invalidated.

I would only add, if I am in orders, if I am a Minister still, and yet not a Minister of the Church of England, of what Church am I a Minister? Whoever is a Minister at all is a Minister of some particular Church. Neither can he cease to be a Minister of that Church, till he is cast out of it by a judicial sentence. Till, therefore, I am so cast out (which I trust will never be) I must style myself a Minister of the Church of England.

6. Your next objection is, "You not only erect Bands which, after the Moravians, you call the *United Society*, but also give out tickets to those that continue in them." These Bands, you think, "have had very bad consequences, as was to be expected, when weak people are made leaders of their brethren, and are set upon expounding Scripture." (*Ibid.*)

You are in some mistakes here. For, (1.) The Bands are not called the *United Society*. (2.) The United Society was originally so called, not after the Moravians, but because it consisted of several smaller societies united together. (3.) Neither the Bands nor the leaders of them, as such, are "set upon expounding Scripture." (4.) The good consequences of their meeting together in Bands, I know. The very bad consequences, I know not.

When any members of these, or of the United Society, are proved to live in known sin, we then mark and avoid them. We separate ourselves from everyone that walks disorderly. Sometimes, if the case be judged infectious (though rarely) this is openly declared. This you style "excommunication," and say, "Does not everyone see a separate ecclesiastical society or communion?" (Page 13.) No. This society does not separate from the communion of the rest of the Church of England. They continue steadfastly with them, both "in the apostolical doctrine, and in the breaking of bread, and in prayers." (Which neither Mr. St— nor Mr. Simpson does, nor the gentleman who writes to you in favour of the Moravians, who also writes urgently to me to separate myself from the Church.) A society "over which you had appointed yourself a governor." No. So far as I governed them, it was at their own request. "And took upon you all the spiritual authority which the very highest Church Governor could claim." What! at Kingswood, in *February*, 1740-1? Not so. I took upon me no authority (then and there at least) than any Steward of a society exerts by the consent of the other members. I did neither more nor less than declare that they who had broken our rules were no longer of our society.

"Can you pretend that you received this authority from our Church?" Not by ordination for I did not exert it as a Priest, but as one whom that society had voluntarily chosen to be at the head of them. "Or that you exercised it in subjection or subordination to her lawful Governors?" I think so. I am sure I did not exercise it in any designed opposition to them. "Did you ever think proper to consult or advise with them, about fixing the terms of your communion?" If you mean, about fixing the rules of admitting or excluding from our society, I never did think it either needful or proper, nor do I at this day.

"How then will you vindicate all these powers?" All these are, "declaring those are no longer of our society." "Here is a manifest congregation. Either it belonged to the Church of England, or not. If it did not, you set up a separate communion against her. And how then are you injured, in being thought to have withdrawn from her?" I have nothing to do with this. The antecedent is false, therefore the consequent falls of course.

"If it did belong to the Church, show where the Church gave you such authority of controlling and regulating it?" Authority of putting disorderly members out of that society? The society itself gave me that authority.

"What private Clergyman can plead her [the Church's] commission to be thus a Judge and Ordinary, even in his own parish." Any Clergyman or layman, without pleading her commission, may be thus a Judge and Ordinary.

"Are not these powers inherent in her Governors and committed to the higher order of her Clergy?" No, not the power of excluding members from a private society, unless on supposition of some such rule as ours is, viz., "That if any man separate from the Church he is no longer a member of our society."

7. But you have more proof yet: "The Grand Jury in Georgia found that you had called yourself Ordinary of Savannah. Nor was this fact contradicted even by those of the Jury who, you say, wrote in your favour. So that it appears you have long had an inclination to be independent and uncontrolled." This argument ought to be good, for it is far fetched. The plain case was this: That Grand Jury did assert that in Mr. Causton's hearing, I had called myself Ordinary of Savannah. The minority of the Jury, in their letter to the Trustees, refuted the other allegations particularly, but thought this one so idle, that they did not deign to give it any farther reply, than, "As to the eighth bill we are in doubt, as not well knowing the meaning of the word *Ordinary*." See (Vol. I. p. 59).

You add, "I appeal to any reasonable man, whether you have not acted as an Ordinary—no, a Bishop—in Kingswood." If you mean in "declaring those disorderly members were no longer of that society," I admit your appeal, whether I acted then as a Bishop or as any Steward of a society may.

"Oh, no, you have gone far beyond the generality of the Dissenters themselves, who do not commit the power of excommunication and appointing to preach [that is another question] to the hands of any private Minister." *The power of excommunication.* True, but this was not excommunication, but a quite different thing.

How far, in what circumstances, and in what sense, I have "appointed men to preach," I have explained at large in the Third Part of the *Farther Appeal*. But I wait for further light, and am ready to consider as I am able, whatever shall be replied to what is there advanced.

8. Your general conclusion is, "Whatever your pretenses or professions may be, you can be looked upon by serious and impartial persons, not as a member—much less a Minister of the Church of England—but as no other than an enemy to her constitution, worship, and doctrine, raising divisions and disturbances in her communion." (*Ibid.* p. 76.) "And yet you say, 'I cannot have greater regard to her

rules.' 'I dare not renounce communion with her.'" (*Ibid.* p. 15.)

I do say so still. I cannot have a greater regard to any human rules, than to follow them in all things, unless where I understand there is a divine rule to the contrary. I dare not renounce communion with the Church of England. As a Minister, I teach her doctrines. I use her offices. I conform to her Rubrics. I suffer reproach for my attachment to her. As a private member, I hold her doctrines. I join in her offices, in prayer, in hearing, in communicating. I expect every reasonable man, concerning these facts, to believe his own eyes and ears. But if these facts are so, how dare any man of common sense charge me with renouncing the Church of England?

9. Use ever so many exaggerations, still the whole of this matter is, (1.) I often use extemporary prayer. (2.) Wherever I can, I preach the gospel. (3.) Those who desire to live the gospel, I advise how to watch over each other, and to put from them such as walk disorderly. Now, whether these things are on other considerations right or wrong, this single point I must still insist on: "All this does not prove, either that I am no member, or that I am no Minister, of the Church of England. Oh, no, nothing can prove I am no member of the Church, till I either am excommunicated, or renounce her communion, and no longer join in her doctrine, and in the breaking of bread, and in prayer. Nor can anything prove I am no Minister of the Church till I either am deposed from my ministry, or voluntarily renounce her, and wholly cease to teach her doctrines, use her offices, and obey her Rubrics for conscience' sake."

However, I grant that whatever is "urged on this topic deserves my most serious consideration." And whenever I am convinced that by taking any methods more or less different from those I now take, I may better "consult the honor of religion, and be able to do more good in the world," by the grace of God I shall not persist in these one hour, but instantly choose the more excellent way.

D. 1. What you urge on the topic of enthusiasm also, I think, "deserves my most serious consideration." You may add, "and presumption." I let it drop once more, because I do not love repetition and because I look upon presumption to be essential to enthusiasm and, consequently, contained therein. I will therefore weigh what you advance concerning it, and explain myself something more at large.

"I am to examine," you say, "how far you have cleared yourself of enthusiasm. My account of this you set down, making as many alterations and omissions as there are lines." (Page 120.) Perhaps more, for I never intended to recite the whole, but only the material part of it. "If you did not wholly approve of it, why would you not let me know what you disliked in it?" Because I do not love many words. Therefore when the argument stood thus, "He that does this is an enthusiast, but you do this," I was generally content with answering the second proposition, and leaving the first as I found it.

"I laid this charge against you and the Methodists in general. Between you every part of the character has been verified." I answer for one. Let the rest answer for themselves, if they have not better employment.

That the question between us may be the more fully understood, I shall briefly compare together, (1.) Your remarks. (2.) My answer. (3.) Your reply, though still I cannot promise to repeat your words at length.

2. You remark, "Though you would be thought an enemy to enthusiasm and presumption, yet in both you are far from being inferior to the Moravians, or indeed to any others." (Page 60.) Strong assertions! *Not inferior to any others*? not to the French Prophets, or John of Leyden! "(1.) Enthusiasm is a false persuasion of an extraordinary divine assistance, which leads men to such conduct as is only to be justified by the supposition of such assistance." I answer, "Before this touches me, you are to prove (which I conceive you have not done yet) that my conduct is such as is only to be justified by the supposition of such assistance." (Page 406.) You reply, "This, I think, is proved in the preceding tract." (Page 120.) I think not. Let men of candor judge. Yet I am persuaded there was such an assistance at some times. You have also to prove that this was a false persuasion.

You remark, (2.) "An enthusiast is, then, sincere but mistaken." (Page 61.) I answered, "That I am mistaken remains to be proved." You reply, "The world must judge." Agreed, if by *the world* you mean men of reason and religion.

You remark, (3.) "His intentions must be good, but his actions will be most abominable." I answered, "What actions of mine are most abominable?" You reply, "The world must be judge, whether your public actions have not been, in *many* respects, abominable." I am glad the charge softens. I hope by and by you will think they are only abominable in some respects.

You remark, (4.) "Instead of making the Word of God the rule of his actions, he follows only secret persuasion or impulse." I answered, "I have declared again and again, that I make the Word of God the rule of all my actions, and that I no more follow any secret impulse instead of it, than I follow Mohammed or Confucius." You reply: "You fall again into your strain of boasting, as if declarations could have any weight against facts. You assert that 'you make the Word of God the rule of all your actions,' and that I 'perhaps do not know many persons.'" (Page 121.)

Stop, Sir. You are stepping over one or two points which I have not done with.

You remark, (5.) "Instead of judging of his spiritual estate by the improvement of his heart, he rests only on ecstasies," etc. I answered, "Neither is this my case. I rest not on them at all. I judge of my spiritual estate by the improvement of my heart and the tenor of my life together." To this I do not perceive you reply one word. Herein, then, I am not an enthusiast.

You remark, (6.) "He is very liable to err, not considering things coolly and carefully." I answered, "So indeed I am. I find it every day more and more. But I do not yet find that this is owing to my lack of 'considering things coolly and carefully.' Perhaps you do not know many persons (excuse my simplicity in speaking it) who more carefully consider every step they take. Yet I know I am not cool or careful enough. May God supply this and all my needs!" (Page 407.) You reply, "Your private life I have nothing to do with," and then enlarge on my "method of consulting Scripture," and of using lots—both of which we will consider by and by. But meantime, observe, that this does not affect the question, for I neither cast lots nor use that method at all till I have considered things with all the care I can. Be this right or wrong, it is no manner of proof that I do not "carefully consider every step I take."

But how little did I profit by begging your excuse, in case I had spoken a word unguardedly! Oh Sir, you put me in mind of him who said, "I know not how to show mercy!" You need never to fight but when you are sure to conquer, seeing you are resolved neither to give nor take quarter.

You remark, (7.) "He is very difficult to be convinced by reason and argument, as he acts upon a supposed principle superior to it—the direction of God's Spirit." I answered, "I am very difficult to be convinced by dry blows or hard names, but not by reason or argument. At least that difficulty cannot spring from the cause you mention. I claim no other direction of God's Spirit than is common to all believers."

You reply, (1.) "I fear this will not be easily reconcilable to your past pretenses and behavior." (Page 124.) I believe it will, in particular to what I speak of the light I received from God in that important affair. (Vol. I. p. 46.) But as to the directions in general of the Spirit of God, we very probably differ in this: You consider those directions to be extraordinary which I suppose to be common to all believers.

You remark, (8.) "Whoever opposes him will be charged with resisting or rejecting the Spirit." I answered, "What! Whoever opposes me, John Wesley? Do I charge every such person with 'rejecting the Spirit?' No more than I charge him with robbing on the highway. Do I charge you with rejecting the Spirit?" You reply, "You deny that you charge the opposers with rejecting the Spirit, and affirm that you never said or thought that what you do is to be accounted the work of God." Here you blend different sentences together, which I must consider apart, as they were written. First, where do I charge you with rejecting the Spirit? If I charge whoever opposes me with this, undoubtedly I charge you. If I do not charge you, that proposition is false. I do not so charge whoever opposes me.

Your next words are, "You affirm that you never said or thought that what you do is to be accounted the work of God. If it is the work of God, you need not deny the other point." Yes, Sir, whether it is or not, I must still deny that I ever charged you with rejecting the Spirit in opposing me.

You remark, (9.) "His own dreams must be regarded as oracles." I answered, "Whose? I desire neither my dreams nor my waking thoughts may be regarded at all, unless just so far as they agree with the oracles of God." To this also you make no reply.

You remark, (10.) "However wild his behavior may be, whatever he does is to be accounted the work of God." It was to this I answered, "I never said so of what I do. I never thought so." This answer was ill expressed, and I might have foreseen you would hardly fail to make your advantage of it. I must therefore explain myself upon it a little farther. You said, "An enthusiast accounts whatever he does to be the work of God." I should have said, "But I do not account whatever I do to be the work of God." What that is which I do account his work will be considered by and by.

You remark, (11.) "He talks in the style of inspired persons." I answered, "No otherwise inspired than you are, if you love God." You reply, "The point was not, whether you are actually inspired, but whether you have talked in the style of those who were so." (Page 126.) That was so much the point, that if it were allowed, it would overturn your whole argument. For if I was inspired (in your sense) you could not term that inspiration enthusiasm without blasphemy. But you again mistake my words. The plain meaning of them is that I talk in the style of those persons who are "no otherwise inspired than you are, if you love God."

You remark, (12.) "He applies Scripture phrases to himself without attending to their original meaning, or once considering the difference of times and circumstances." (Page 62.) I answered "I am not conscious of anything like this. I apply no Scripture phrase either to myself or any other without carefully considering both the original meaning, and the secondary sense where, allowing for different times and circumstances, it may be applied to ordinary Christians." (Page 407.) You reply, "This also you deny to have done, holding however, some secondary sense (what it is you have not told us) in which Scripture phrases may be applied to ordinary Christians." I have largely told you what I mean by a secondary sense, in the First Part of the *Farther Appeal*. You add, "Many things which were truly written of the preaching of Christianity at first you have vainly applied to yourselves." Sir, I am to answer only for myself, as I will for that expression, "Behold the day of the Lord is come. He is again visiting and redeeming his people!"

3. I come now to what you discourse upon at large, as the two grand instances of my enthusiasm. The first is plainly this: At some rare times, when I have been in great distress of soul, or in utter uncertainty how to act in an important case which required a speedy determination, after using all other means that occurred, I have cast lots or opened the Bible. And by this means I have been relieved from that distress or directed in that uncertainty.

Instances of this kind occur in pages 12, 14, 15, 28, and 88 of the third *Journal*; also in pages 27, 28, and 80 of the last *Journal*.[3] I desire any who would understand this matter thoroughly to read those passages as they stand at length.

As to the particular instances, I would observe, (1.) That with regard to my first journey to Bristol, you should in any case, have set down those words that preface the scriptures there recited: "I was begged, in the most pressing manner, to come to Bristol without delay. This I was not at all eager to do—and perhaps a little the less inclined to it—because of the remarkable scriptures which were offered, as often as we inquired, concerning the consequence of this removal. Whether this was permitted only for the trial of our faith, God knows and the event will show." From the scriptures afterwards recited, some inferred that the event they concerned was yet afar off. I infer nothing at all. I still know not how to judge, but leave the whole to God. This only I know, that the continual expectation of death was then an unspeakable blessing to me. I did not dare, knowingly, to waste a moment, neither to throw away one desire on earthly things, those words being ever uppermost in my thoughts, and indeed frequently on my tongue:

> *Ere long, when sovereign wisdom wills,*
> *My soul an unknown path shall tread,*
> *Shall strangely leave, who strangely fills*
> *This frame, and waft me to the dead.*

> *O, what is death? 'Tis life's last shore,*
> *Where vanities are vain no more;*
> *Where all pursuits their goal obtain,*
> *And life is all retouch'd again.*

I observe, (2.) That in two other of those instances, (Vol. I. pp. 163, 165,) it is particularly mentioned that "I was troubled," and that by the seasonable application of those scriptures that trouble was entirely removed. The same blessing I received (so I must term it still) from the words set down in page 231, and in a yet higher degree from that exceeding apposite scripture mentioned in Vol. I, page 307.

I observe, (3.) That at the times to which your other citations refer, I was utterly uncertain how to act in points of great importance, and such as required a speedy determination. By this means my uncertainty was removed, and I went on my way rejoicing. (Vol. I. pp. 163, 165, 264.)

My own experience, therefore, which you think should discourage me for the future from anything of this kind does, on the contrary, greatly encourage me herein. I have found much benefit and no inconvenience, unless perhaps, this is one, that you "cannot acquit me of enthusiasm." Add, if you please, "and presumption."

But you ask, "Has God ever commanded us to do thus?" I believe he has neither commanded nor forbidden it in Scripture. But then remember, "that Scripture [to use the words which you cite from "our learned and judicious Hooker"] is not the only rule of all things which, in this life, may be done by men." All I affirm concerning this is that it may be done, and that I have, in fact, received assistance and direction thereby.

4. I give the same answer to your assertion, that we are not ordered in Scripture to decide any points in question by lots. (*Remarks*, p. 123) You admit, indeed, there are instances of this in Scripture, but you affirm, "These were miraculous, nor can we, without presumption [a species of enthusiasm] apply this method." I want proof of this. Bring one plain text of Scripture, and I am satisfied. "This, I understand, you learned from the Moravians." I did, though it is true Mr. Whitefield thought I went too far in this.

"Instances of the same occur in your *Journals*. I will mention only one. It being debated when you should go to Bristol, you say, 'We at length all agreed to decide it by lot, and by this it was determined I should go.' (Vol. I. p. 176.) Is this your way of carefully considering every step you take? Can there be greater rashness and extravagance? Reason is thus in a manner rendered useless, prudence is set aside, and affairs of importance left to be determined by chance!" (*Remarks*, p. 124.)

So this you give as a genuine instance of my proceedings, and I suppose of your own fairness and candor! "We agreed, at length, to decide it by lot." True, *at length*; after a debate of some hours; after carefully hearing and weighing coolly all the reasons which could be alleged on either side. Our brethren still continuing the dispute, without any probability of their coming to one conclusion, we at length (the night being now far spent) all agreed to this. "Can there be greater rashness and extravagance?" I cannot help but think there can. "Reason is thus in a manner rendered useless." No, we had used it as far as it could go, from Saturday, March 17 (when I received the first letter) to Wednesday, 28, when the case was laid before the society.

"Prudence is set aside." Not so, but the arguments here were so equal that she saw not how to determine. "And affairs of importance left to be determined by chance!" *By chance!* What a blunder then, is that, "The lot is cast into the lap, but the whole disposal thereof is of the Lord!"

This, I firmly believe, is truth and reason, and will be to the end of the world. I therefore still subscribe to that declaration of the Moravian Church, laid before the whole body of Divines in the University of Wirtemberg, and not by them counted as enthusiasm: "We have a peculiar esteem for lots and accordingly use them, both in public and private, to decide points of importance, when the reasons brought on each side appear to be of equal weight. We believe this to be then the only way of wholly setting aside our own will, of acquitting ourselves of all blame, and clearly knowing what is the will of God." (Vol. I. p 146.)

5. You next remarked several instances of my "enthusiasm." The first was that of Mrs. Jones. The next ran thus: "Again, you say, 'I expounded out of the fullness that was given me.'" (*Remarks*, p. 64.) I answered, "I mean, I had then a fuller, deeper sense of what I spoke than I ordinarily have." (Page 409) But if you still think "it would have been more decent to have said, 'According to the best of my power and ability, with God's assistance, I expounded,'" I will say so another time.

With regard to the third instance of enthusiasm, you remarked, "If you would not have us look on this as miraculous, there is nothing in it worthy of being related." (*Remarks*, p. 64.) I answered, "It may be so. Let it pass then, as a trifle not worth relating. Still it is no proof of enthusiasm. For I would not have you look upon it as miraculous, but as a remarkable instance of God's particular providence." (Page 909) How friendly and generous is your reply! "You seem ashamed of it. I am glad you give this fooling up, and hope for the future you will treat your readers better." (*Second Letter*, p. 131.) Sir, I am not ashamed of it, nor shall I ever "give this fooling up" till I give up the Bible. I still look upon this "as a remarkable instance of God's particular providence."

But "how is this consistent with admitting it to be a trifle?" (*Ibid*. p. 132.) My words do not imply that I admit it so to be. Being urged with the dilemma, "Either this is related as miraculous [and then it is enthusiasm] or it is not worth relating." I answered (to avoid drawing the saw of controversy) "Let it pass, then, as a trifle not worth relating. Still [if it is a trifle, which I suppose, not grant] it is no proof of enthusiasm. For I would not have you look upon it as miraculous."

And yet I believe I yielded too much, and what might too much favour your assertion that "there is a great difference between particular providences and such extraordinary interpositions." Please, Sir, show me what this difference is. It is a subject that deserves your coolest thoughts. "I know no ground to hope or pray for such immediate reliefs. These things must be represented either as common accidents or as miracles." I do not thoroughly understand your terms. What is a common accident— that a sparrow falls to the ground, or something more inconsiderable than the hairs of your head? Is there no medium between accident and miracle? If there is, what is that medium? When we are agreed with regard to these few points, I shall be glad to resume the subject.

6. The fourth instance of my enthusiasm was this, that I "related judgments inflicted on my opposers." As to Mr. Molther, I must observe once more that I do believe there was a particular providence in his sickness. But I do not believe (nor did I intend to insinuate) that it was a judgment for opposing me.

You go on. "Again you mention 'as an awful providence, the case of a poor wretch who was last week cursing and blaspheming, and had boasted to many that he would come again on Sunday, and no man should stop his mouth then. But on Friday God laid his hand upon him, and on Sunday he was buried.'" (*Remarks*, p. 66.) I answered, "I look on this as a manifest judgment of God on a hardened sinner for his complicated wickedness." (Page 410.) You reply, "Add, if you please, 'His laboring with all his might to hinder the Word of God.' Here therefore is a confessed judgment for his opposition to you." (*Second Letter*, p. 133) There is, for his thus opposing with curses and blasphemy. This was part of his complicated wickedness. Here then you "think I plead guilty." Not of enthusiasm till you prove this was not "an awful providence."

"Again: 'One was just going to beat his wife (which he frequently did) when God smote him in a moment, so that his hand dropped and he fell down upon the ground, having no more strength than a newborn child.' Have we any warrant either from Scripture or the common dispensations of providence to interpret misfortunes of this nature as judgments?" (*Remarks*, p. 67.) I answered, "Can you, Sir, consider this as one of the common dispensations of providence? Have you known a parallel one in your life? But it was never cited by me (as it is by you) as an immediate punishment on a man for *opposing me*." (Pages 409, 410) You reply, "As if what is not common, or what I have not known, must be a miraculous judgment." I believe it was, whether miraculous or not, a judgment mixed with mercy.

You now add to the rest the following instance: "One John Haydon, a man of a regular life and conversation, being informed that people fell into strange fits at the societies, came to see and judge for himself. But he was still less satisfied than before, so that he went about to his acquaintances one after another, and labored above measure to convince them it was a delusion of the devil. We were going home, when one met us in the street, and informed us that J. H. was fallen raving mad. It seems he had sat down to dinner, but had a mind first to end the sermon on *Salvation by Faith*. In reading the last page, he changed color, fell off his chair, and began screaming terribly and beating himself against the ground. The neighbors were alarmed and flocked into the house.

I came in and found him upon the floor, the room being full of people, whom his wife would have kept without. But he cried aloud, 'No, let them all come. Let all the world see the just judgment of God.' Two or three men were holding him as well as they could. He immediately fixed his eyes upon me and cried, 'Yes, this is he, who I said was a deceiver of the people. But God has overtaken me. I said it was all a delusion. But this is no delusion.' He then roared out, 'Oh, you devil! You cursed devil! Oh, yes, you legion of devils! You cannot stay! Christ will cast you out. I know His work is begun. Tear me to pieces if you will, but you cannot hurt me.' He then beat himself against the ground again, his breast heaving at the same time as in the pangs of death, and great drops of sweat trickling down his face. We all went to prayer. His pangs ceased, and both his body and soul were set at liberty." (Vol. 1. p. 190.)

If you had pleased, you might have added from the next paragraph, "Returning to J. H., we found his voice was lost and his body weak as that of an infant. But his soul was in peace, full of love, and rejoicing in hope of the glory of God."

You add, "This you may desire, for all I know, to pass as a trifle too." (*Remarks*, p. 134.) No. It is so terrible an instance of the judgment of God (though at length "mercy rejoiced over judgment") as ought never to be forgotten by those who fear God, so long as the sun or moon endures.

7. The account of people down in fits you cite as a fifth instance of my enthusiasm. It is "plain," you say, that I "look upon both the disorders, and the removals of them, to be supernatural." (*Remarks*, p. 67) I answered, "It is not quite plain. I look upon some of these cases as wholly natural; on the rest, as mixed. Both the disorders and the removals are partly natural and partly not." (Page 410.) You reply, "It would have been kind to have let us know your rule by which you distinguish these." I will. I distinguish them by the circumstances that precede, accompany, and follow. "However, some of these you here allow to be in part supernatural. Miracles, therefore, are not wholly ceased." Can you prove they are, by Scripture or reason?

You then refer to two or three cases, related in Vol. I. pp. 188, 189. I believe there was a supernatural power on the minds of the persons there mentioned, which occasioned their bodies to be so affected by the natural laws of the vital union. This point, therefore, you have to prove, or here is no enthusiasm; that there was no supernatural power in the case.

On this you remarked, "You leave no room to doubt that you would have these cases considered as those of the demoniacs in the New Testament in order, I suppose, to parallel your supposed cures of them with those highest miracles of Christ and his disciples, the casting out devils." (*Remarks*, p. 63.) I answered, "I should once have wondered at your making such a supposition, but now I wonder at nothing of the kind." You reply, "Why so? What have I done lately, to take off your surprise? Have I forfeited my character for innocent and fair-dealing with you?" (*Second Letter*, p. 135.) Since you ask me the question, I will answer it, I hope in love, and in the spirit of meekness. I scarcely know, of all who have written against me, a less innocent dealer; or one who has shown a more steady, invariable disposition to put an ill construction on whatever I say.

"But why would you not particularly explain these cases?" I will explain myself upon them once for all. For more than three hundred years after Christ, you know, demoniacs were common in the Church. I suppose you are not uninformed, that during this period (if not much longer) they were continually relieved by the prayers of the faithful. Nor can I doubt but demoniacs will remain, so long as Satan is the "god of this world." I doubt not there are such at this day. I believe John Haydon was one, but of whatever sort his disorder was, that it was removed by prayer is undeniable.

Now, Sir, you have only two points to prove, and then your argument will be conclusive: (1.) That to think or say, "There are demoniacs now, and they are now relieved by prayer," is enthusiasm. (2.) That to say, "Demoniacs were or are relieved, on prayer made by Cyprian, or their parish Minister," is to parallel the actions of Cyprian or that Minister with the highest miracles of Christ and his disciples.

8. You remarked, "It will be difficult to persuade any sober person that there is anything supernatural in these disorders." (*Remarks*, p. 69) The remainder of that paragraph I abridged thus: You attempt to account for those fits by "obstructions or irregularities of the blood and spirits; hysterical disorders, watchings, fastings, closeness of rooms, great crowds, violent heat," and lastly by "terrors, perplexities and doubts in weak and well-meaning men, which," you think, "in many of the cases before us, have quite overset their understandings." (*Remarks*, p. 43.)

I answered, "As to each of the rest, let it go as far as it can go." (Let it be supposed to have some influence in some cases, perhaps fully to account for one in a thousand.) "But I require proof of the last way by which you would account for these disorders." Why, "the instances," you say, "of religious madness have much increased since you began to disturb the world." I doubt the fact. You reply, "This no way disproves it." (*Second Letter*, p. 137.) Yes, it does, till you produce some proof, for a bare negation is the proper and sufficient answer to a bare affirmation.

I add, "If these instances had increased daily, it is easy to account for them another way," as is done in the First Part of the *Farther Appeal*, at the one hundred thirty-first and following pages.

You say, "Most have heard of or known several of the Methodists thus driven to distraction." I answered, "You may have heard of five hundred but how many have you known? Be pleased to name eight or ten of them. I cannot find them, no, not one of them to this day, either man, woman, or child." (Page 411) You reply, "This [the naming them] would be very improper and unnecessary." (*Second Letter*, p. 138) However, Sir, it is extremely necessary that you should name them to me in private. I will then, if required, excuse you to the public. Till then I cannot do so.

The person I mentioned, whom you threw into much doubt and perplexity, then lived in the parish of St. Ann, Westminster. I related the case just as she related it to me. But she is able and ready to answer for herself.

9. You go on: "It is the most charitable supposition we can make, that many of the cases you have mentioned in your *Journals*, and some of which have been represented above, are of this kind," that is, instances of madness. (*Second Letter*, p. 138.) Oh tender charity! But cannot your charity reach one hair's breadth farther than this? No. For "otherwise [that is, if those persons were not mad] the presumption and despair are terrible indeed." But what if you were to suppose John Haydon (for one instance) was not mad, but under a temporary possession, and that others were deeply convinced of sin, and of the wrath of God abiding on them? I should think this supposition (be it true or false) was fully as charitable as the other.

I said, "I cannot find one such instance to this day." You reply, "Yet once you could not help but be under some concern with regard to one or two persons, who seemed to be indeed lunatic, as well as sorely vexed." So they seemed, but it soon appeared they were not. The very next paragraph mentions that one of these, within a few hours, was "filled with the spirit of love and of a sound mind." (Vol. I. p. 231.)

But you are resolved, come what will, to win this point; and so add, "Toward the end of your *Farther Appeal* (First Part, p. 131) you say you have seen one instance of real, lasting madness. This was one whom you took with you to Bristol, who was afterwards prejudiced against you, and began a vehement invective both against your person and doctrines. In the midst of this he was struck raving mad." Add, "And so he continued till his friends put him into Bedlam, and probably blamed his madness on me ." If they did not, it is now done to their hands.

10. "As to the cure of these fits, I observed [so you, p. 139, proceed] that you had frequently represented them as miraculous, as the instantaneous consequences of your prayers." My former answer to this was, "I have set down the facts just as they were, passing no judgment upon them myself, and leaving every man else to judge as he pleases."

I am glad you give me an occasion of reviewing this answer. Upon reflection, I do not like it at all. It grants you more than I can in conscience do. As it can be proved by abundance of witnesses that these cures were frequently (indeed almost always) the instantaneous consequences of prayer, your inference is just. I cannot, dare not affirm, that they were purely natural. I believe they were not. I believe many of them were accomplished by the supernatural power of God, that of John Haydon in particular, (I focus on this, and will debate you upon it when you please.) Yet this is not barefaced enthusiasm. Nor can you prove it to be any enthusiasm at all unless you can prove that this is falsely ascribed to supernatural power.

"The next case," you say, "relates to the spotted fever, which you represent as being extremely fatal; but you believe there was not one with whom you were associated but recovered. I admitted that here is no intimation of anything miraculous." (*Remarks*, p. 72) "You ask, 'Why then is this cited as an instance of my enthusiasm?' (Page 412.) You surely cannot think that false pretences to miracles are the whole of enthusiasm." No, but I think they are that part of enthusiasm which you here tried to prove. You are here to prove that I "boast of curing bodily ills by prayer, without the use of other means." (*Remarks*, p. 71) But if there is no intimation in my account of anything miraculous, or that proper remedies had not been applied, how is this a proof that I boast of curing bodily ills without applying any remedies at all?

"But you seem to desire to have it believed that an extraordinary blessing attended your prayers. If the circumstances could be particularly inquired into, most probably it would appear that either the fury of the illness was abated, or the persons you visited were seized with it in a more favourable degree, or were by reason of a good constitution more capable of going through it. Neither do I believe that they would have failed of an equal blessing and success had they had the assistance and prayers of their own parish Ministers."

There, Sir. Now I have done as you require. I have quoted our whole remark. But does all this prove that I "boast of curing bodily ills by prayer without the use of any other means?" If you say, Although it does not prove this, it proves that "you seem to desire to have it believed that an extraordinary blessing attended your prayers," and this is another sort of enthusiasm—it is very well. So it does not prove the conclusion you intended, but it proves another which is as good!

11. The two last instances of my enthusiasm which you bring (*Remarks*, pp. 72, 73) I had summed up in two lines, thus: "At two different times, being ill and in violent pain, I prayed to God and found immediate ease." (*Answer*, p. 412) But you say, I "must not hope to escape so. These instances must once more be laid before me particularly," (*Second Letter*, p. 140) I must yield to necessity and set them down from the beginning to the end.

"Saturday, March 21. I explained in the evening the thirty-third chapter of Ezekiel; in applying which, I was seized with such a pain in my side I could not speak. I knew my remedy and immediately kneeled down. In a moment the pain was gone." (Vol. I. p. 304.)

"Friday, May 8. I found myself much out of order. However, I arranged to preach in the evening. But on Saturday my bodily strength failed, so that for several hours I could scarcely lift up my head. Sunday, 10. I was obliged to lie down most part of the day, being easy only in that posture. In the evening,—beside the pain in my back and head and the fever which still continued upon me—just as I began to pray I was seized with such a cough that I could hardly speak. At the same time it came strongly into my mind, 'These signs shall follow them that believe.' I called on Jesus aloud to 'increase my faith,' and to 'confirm the word of his grace.' While I was speaking my pain vanished away, the fever left me, my bodily strength returned, and for many weeks I felt neither weakness or pain. Unto you, Oh Lord, do I give thanks." (*Ibid*. p. 310.)

When you first cited these as proofs of enthusiasm, I answered, "I will put your argument into this form: "He that believes those are miraculous cures which are not so, is a rank enthusiast, You believe those are miraculous cures which are not so. Therefore, you are a rank enthusiast.

"What do you mean by miraculous? If you term everything so, which is 'not strictly accountable for by the ordinary course of natural causes,' then I deny the latter part of the minor proposition. And unless you can make this good — unless you can prove the effects in question are 'strictly accountable for by the ordinary course of natural causes'— your argument is worth nothing."

You reply, "Your answer to the objection is very evasive, though you pretend to put my argument in form. You mistake the major proposition, which should have been:

"He that represents those cures as the immediate effects of his own prayers—and as miraculous—which are not so, is a rank enthusiast, if sincere:

"'But this you have done: *Ergo*, etc.'"

To this clumsy reasoning I rejoin, (1.) The words "if sincere" are utterly irrelevant. If insincerity is supposed, enthusiasm will be out of the question. (2.) Those words "as the effects of his own prayers" may likewise be pared off. They are unnecessary and cumbersome, the argument being complete without them. (3.) With or without them, the proposition is false, unless so far as it coincides with that you reject. It is the believing those to be miracles which are not that constitutes an enthusiast, not the representing them one way or the other, unless so far as it implies such a belief.

12. Upon my answer to the reasoning first proposed you observe, "Thus [by denying the latter part of the minor] you clear yourself from the charge of enthusiasm, by acknowledging the cures to be supernatural and miraculous. Why then would you not speak out and directly say that you can work real and undoubted miracles? This would put the controversy between you and your opposers on a short foot and be an effective proof of the truth of your pretences." (*Second Letter*, p. 142.)

E. 1. I have in some measure explained myself on the topic of miracles in the Third Part of the *Farther Appeal*. But since you repeat the demand (though without taking any notice of the arguments there advanced) I will endeavour once more to give you a distinct, full, and precise answer.

(1.) I acknowledge that I have seen with my eyes and heard with my ears several things which, to the best of my judgment, cannot be accounted for by the ordinary course of natural causes. I therefore believe these ought to be "ascribed to the extraordinary interposition of God." If any man chooses to style these *miracles*, I do not change the claim. I have diligently inquired into the facts. I have weighed the preceding and following circumstances. I have striven to account for them in a natural way. I could not, without doing violence to my reason. Not to go far back, I am clearly persuaded that the sudden deliverance of John Haydon was one instance of this kind. My own recovery on May 10th was another. I cannot account for either of these in a natural way. Therefore I believe they were both supernatural.

(2.) I must observe that the truth of these facts is supported by the same kind of proof as that of all other facts is accustomed to be, namely, the testimony of competent witnesses. The testimony here is in as high a degree as any reasonable man can desire. Those witnesses were many in number. They could not be deceived themselves, for the facts in question they saw with their own eyes and heard with their own ears. Nor is it credible that so many of them would combine together with a view of deceiving others. The greater part were men that feared God, as appeared by the general tenor of their lives.

In the case of John Haydon, this thing was not contrived and executed in a corner, and in the presence of his own family only, or three or four persons prepared for the purpose. No, it was in an open street of the city of Bristol, at one or two in the afternoon. The doors being all open from the beginning, not only many of the neighbours from every side but several others (indeed whosoever desired it) went in till the house could contain no more.

Nor yet does the account of my own illness and recovery depend, as you suppose, on my bare word. There were many witnesses both of my disorder on Friday and Saturday, and of my lying down most part of Sunday. They were well satisfied this could not be the effect of a slight indisposition. All who saw me that evening plainly discerned (what I could not wholly conceal) that I was in pain. About two hundred of them were present when I was seized with that cough, which cut me short so that I could speak no more, till I cried out aloud, "Lord, increase my faith! Lord, confirm the word of thy grace!" The same persons saw and heard that at that instant I changed my posture and broke out into thanksgiving; that quickly after I stood upright (which I could not before) and showed no more sign either of sickness or pain.

Yet I must desire you well to observe, Thirdly, that my will, or choice, or desire, had no place either in this or any case of this kind that has ever fallen under my notice. Five minutes before, I had no thought of this. I expected nothing less. I was willing to wait for a gradual recovery in the ordinary use of outward means. I did not look for any other cure till the moment before I found it.

It is my belief that the case was always the same with regard to the most "real and undoubted miracles." I believe God never interposed his miraculous power but according to his own sovereign will. It was not according to the will of man, neither of him by whom he worked, nor of any other man whatever. The wisdom as well as the power are his. Nor can I find that ever, from the beginning of the world, he lodged this power in any mere man to be used whenever that man saw good.

Suppose there was a man now on earth who did work "real and undoubted miracles." I would ask, By whose power does he work these, and at whose pleasure — his own, or God's? Not his own, but God's. But if so, then your demand is not on man, but on God. I cannot say it is modest thus to challenge God, or well suiting the relation of a creature to his Creator.

2. However, I cannot help but think there have been already so many plain interventions of divine power as will shortly leave you without excuse, if you either deny or despise them. We desire no favour, but the justice that diligent inquiry may be made concerning them. We are ready to name the persons on whom that power was shown which belongs to none but God (not one or two, or ten or twelve only) and to point out their places of living. We believe they shall answer every pertinent question, fairly and directly, and if required shall give all those answers upon oath before any who are empowered so to receive them. It is our particular request that the circumstances which went before, which accompanied, and which followed after the facts under consideration may be thoroughly examined and punctually noted down. Let this be done (and is it not highly needful it should, at least by those who would form an exact judgment) and we have no fear that any reasonable man should hesitate to say, "This, God has done!"

As there have been already so many instances of this kind, far beyond what we had dared to ask or think, I cannot take upon me to say whether or not it will please God to add to their number. I have not in this "known the mind of the Lord," neither am I "his counsellor." He may, or he may not. I cannot affirm or deny. I have no light, and I have no desire either way. "It is the Lord Let him do what seems good to him." I desire only to be as clay in his hand.

3. But what if there were now to be done ever so many "real and undoubted miracles?" (I suppose you mean by *undoubted* such as being sufficiently attested, ought not to be doubted of.) Why, "This," you say, "would put the controversy on a short foot, and be an effective

proof of the truth of your pretences." By no means. As common as this assertion is, there is none upon earth more false. Suppose a teacher were now, on this very day, to work "real and undoubted miracles." This would extremely little "shorten the controversy" between him and the greater part of his opposers. All this would not force them to believe. Many would still stand just where they did before. Since men may "harden their hearts" against miracles as well as against arguments.

So men have done from the beginning of the world, even against such remarkable, glorious miracles, against such interventions of the power of God, as may not be again till the completion of all things. Permit me to remind you only of a few instances, and to observe that the argument holds *à fortiori*. Who will ever be impowered of God again to work such miracles as these were? Did Pharaoh look on all that Moses and Aaron performed as an "effective proof of the truth of their pretences?" even when "the Lord made the sea dry land, and the waters were divided;" when "the children of Israel went into the midst of the sea, and the waters were a wall unto them on the right hand, and on the left?" (Exod. 14: 21, 22.) Oh, no,

> *The wounded dragon raged in vain;*
> *And, fierce the utmost plague to brave,*
> *Madly he dared the parted main,*
> *And sunk beneath the o'erwhelming wave.*

Was all this "an effective proof of the truth of their pretences," to the Israelites themselves? It was not. "They were" still "disobedient at the sea; even at the Red Sea!" Was the giving them day by day "bread from heaven" "an effective proof" to those "two hundred and fifty princes of the assembly, famous in the congregation, men of renown," who said, with Dathan and Abiram, "Wilt thou put out the eyes of these men? We will not come up?" (Numbers 16: 14) Oh, no, "when the ground clave asunder that was under them; and the earth opened her mouth and swallowed them up?" (Verse 32.) Neither was this an "effective proof" to those who saw it with their eyes, and heard the cry of those that went down into the pit. The very next day they "murmured against Moses and against Aaron, saying, Ye have killed the people of the Lord!" (Verse 41.)

Was not the case generally the same with regard to the Prophets that followed? Several of them "stopped the mouths of lions, quenched the violence of fire," did many mighty works. Yet their own people received them not. Yet "they were stoned, they were sawn asunder, they were slain with the sword." They were "destitute, afflicted, tormented!" utterly contrary to the commonly received supposition, that working real, undoubted miracles must bring all controversy to an end, and convince every disbeliever.

Let us come nearer yet. How stood the case between our Lord himself and his opposers? Did he not work "real and undoubted miracles?" And what was the effect? Still, when "he came to his own, his own received him not." Still "he was despised and rejected of men." Still it was a challenge not to be answered: "Have any of the rulers or of the Pharisees believed on him?" After this, how can you imagine, that whoever works miracles must convince "all men of the truth of his pretences?"

I would just remind you of only one instance more. "There sat a certain man at Lystra, impotent in his feet, being a cripple from his mother's womb, who never had walked. The same heard Paul speak; who steadfastly beholding him, and perceiving that he had faith to be healed, said, with a loud voice, Stand upright on thy feet. And he leaped and walked." Here was so undoubted a miracle that the people "lifted up their voices, saying, The gods are come down in the likeness of men." But how long were even these convinced of the truth of his pretences? Only till "there came thither certain Jews from Antioch and Iconium." and then they stoned him (as they supposed) to death! (Acts 14: 8, etc.) So certain it is, that no miracles whatever which were ever yet worked in the world, were effective to prove the most glaring truth to those that hardened their hearts against it.

4. And it will equally hold in every age and nation. "If they hear not Moses and the Prophets, neither will they be" convinced of what they desire not to believe, "though one rose from the dead." Without a miracle, without one rising from the dead, $εαν$ $τις$ $θελη$ $το$ $θελημα$ $αυτου$ $ποιειν$, "if any man be willing to do his will, he shall know of the doctrine, whether it be of God." But if he is not willing to do his will, he will never need an excuse, a plausible reason, for rejecting it, oh, yes, though ever so many miracles were performed to confirm it. For let ever so much

"light come into the world," it will have no effect (such is the wise and just will of God) on those who "love darkness rather than light." It will not convince those who do not simply desire to do the will of their Father which is in heaven; those who mind earthly things; who (if they do not continue in any gross outward sin, yet) love pleasure or ease; yet seek profit or power, promotion or reputation. Nothing will ever be an effective proof to these of the holy and acceptable will of God, unless first their proud hearts are humbled, their stubborn wills bowed down, and their desires brought, at least in some degree, into obedience to the law of Christ.

Therefore, although it should please God to work anew all the wonders that ever were worked on the earth, still these men, however "wise and prudent" they may be in things relating to the present world, would fight against God and all his messengers in spite of all these miracles. Meanwhile, God will reveal his truth to babies, to those who are meek and lowly, whose desires are in heaven, who want to "know nothing save Jesus Christ and him crucified." These need no outward miracle to show them his will. They have a plain rule—the written Word. And "the anointing which they have received of him abideth in them, and teacheth them of all things." (1 John 2: 27) Through this they are enabled to bring all doctrines "to the law and to the testimony." Whatever is agreeable to this they receive without waiting to see it attested by miracles. On the other hand, whatever is contrary to this they reject, nor can any miracles move them to receive it.

5. Yet I do not know that God has in any way precluded himself from thus exerting his sovereign power, from working miracles in any kind or degree, in any age, to the end of the world. I do not recollect any scripture where we are taught that miracles were to be confined within the limits either of the Apostolic or the Cyprianic Age, or of any period of time, longer or shorter, even till the restitution of all things. I have not observed, either in the Old Testament or the New, any intimation at all of this kind.

St. Paul says indeed, once, concerning two of the miraculous gifts of the Spirit (so I think that text is usually understood) "Whether there be prophecies, they shall fail; whether there be tongues, they shall cease." But he does not say either that these or any other miracles shall cease, till faith and hope shall cease also; till they are all swallowed up in the vision of God, and love is all in all.

I presume you will agree there is one kind of miracles (loosely speaking) which have not ceased, namely τερατα ψευδους, "lying wonders," diabolical miracles, or works beyond the virtue of natural causes, performed by the power of evil spirits. Nor can you easily conceive that these will cease as long as the father of lies is the prince of this world. And why should you think that the God of truth is less active than him, or that he will not have his miracles also? It is not as man wills neither when he wills; but according to his own excellent wisdom and greatness.

6. But even if it were supposed that God does now work beyond the operation of merely natural causes, yet what impression would this make on you in the disposition your mind is now in? Suppose the trial were repeated, were made again tomorrow. One informs you the next day, "While a clergyman was preaching yesterday where I was, a man came who had been long ill of an incurable disease. Prayer was made for him, and he was restored to perfect health."

Suppose, now, that this were real fact. Perhaps you would scarcely have patience to hear the account of it, but would cut it short in the midst of the narration with, "Do you tell this as something supernatural? Then miracles have not ceased."

But if you should venture to ask, "Where was this, and who was the person that prayed?" and it was answered, "At the Foundery near Moorfields. The person who prayed was Mr. Wesley," what a dampening of your spirits comes at once! What a weight falls on your mind at the very first! It is well if you have any heart or desire to move one step further. If you should, what a strong additional inclination do you now feel to deny the fact! And is there not a ready excuse for so doing? "O, they who tell the story are doubtless his own people, most of whom, we may be sure, will say anything for him. The rest will believe anything."

But if you at length allowed the fact, might you not find ways to account for it by natural causes? "Great crowds, violent heat, with obstructions and irregularities of the blood and spirits," will do wonders. If you could not help but allow it was more than natural, might not some plausible reason be found for ranking it among the lying wonders, for ascribing it to the devil rather than God?

If, after all, you were convinced it was the finger of God, must you not still bring every doctrine advanced to the law and to the testimony, the only sure and infallible test of all? What, then, is the use of this continual demand, "Show us a sign, and we will believe?" What will you believe? I hope no more than is written in the Book of God. And thus far you might venture to believe, even without a miracle.

7. Let us consider this point yet a little farther. "What is it you would have us prove by miracles?—the doctrines we preach?" We prove these by Scripture and reason, and if need be, by history. What else is it, then, that we are to prove by miracles? At length we have a distinct reply: "Wise and sober men will not otherwise be convinced [that is, unless you prove this by miracles] that God is, by the means of such teachers and such doctrines, working a great and extraordinary work in the earth." (*Preface*, p. 6)

So then the precise point which you, in their name, call upon us to prove by miracles is this: "that God is, by these teachers, working a great and extraordinary work in the earth."

What I mean by "a great and extraordinary work" is the bringing multitudes of great, notorious sinners, in a short space, to the fear, and love, and service of God, to an entire change of heart and life.

Now, then, let us take a nearer view of the proposition, and see which part of it we are to prove by miracles.

"Is it, (1.) That A. B. was for many years without God in the world, a common swearer, a drunkard, a Sabbath-breaker?

"Or, (2.) that he is not so now?

"Or, (3.) that he continued so till he heard these men preach, and from that time was another man?

"Not so. The proper way to prove these facts is, by the testimony of competent witnesses. And these witnesses are ready whenever required to give full evidence of them.

"Or would you have us prove by miracles, (4.) That this was not done by our own power or holiness — that God only is able to raise the dead, to revive those who are dead in trespasses and sins?"

Surely not. Whosoever believes the Scriptures will want no new proof of this.

Where then is the wisdom of those men who demand miracles in proof of such a proposition? One branch, "that such sinners were reformed by the means of these Teachers," is a plain fact and can only be proved by testimony, as all other facts are. The other branch, "That this is a work of God, a great and more-than-ordinary work," needs no proof, as carrying its own evidence to every thinking man.

8. To sum this up: No truly wise or sober man can possibly desire or expect miracles to prove either, (1.) that these doctrines are true—this must be decided by Scripture and reason; or (2.) that these facts are true — this can only be proved by testimony; or (3.) that to change sinners from darkness to light is the work of God alone, only using what instruments he pleases—this is glaringly self-evident; or (4.) that such a change made in so many notorious sinners, within so short a time, is a great and extraordinary work of God. This also carries its own evidence.

What then is it which remains to be proved by miracles? Perhaps you will say it is this: "That God has called or sent you to do this." Oh, no, this is implied in the third of the foregoing propositions. If God has actually used us in it, if his work has in fact prospered in our hands, then he has called or sent us to do this. I ask reasonable men to weigh this thoroughly, whether the fact does not plainly prove the call; whether He who enables us thus to save souls alive, does not commission us so to do. By giving us power to "pluck these brands out of the burning," does He not authorize us to exert it?

Oh, that it were possible for you to consider calmly whether the success of the gospel of Jesus Christ, even as it is preached by us, the least of his servants, is not itself a miracle, never to be forgotten! It is one which cannot be denied, as being visible at this day, not in one, but a hundred places, It is one which cannot be accounted for by the ordinary course of any natural cause whatever, one which cannot be ascribed, with any colour of reason, to diabolical agency. Lastly, it is one which will bear the infallible test,—the trial of the written Word.

F. 1. But here I am aware of abundance of objections. You object that to speak anything of myself, of what I have done, or am doing now, is mere boasting and vanity. This complaint you frequently repeat. So, p. 102: "The following page is full of boasting." "You boast very much of the numbers you have converted;" (p. 113) and again, "As to myself, I hope I shall never be led to imitate you in boasting." I think therefore it is necessary, once for all, to examine this accusation thoroughly, and to show distinctly what that good thing is which you disguise under this bad name.

(a.) From the year 1725 to 1729 I preached much, but saw no fruit of my labour. Indeed it could not be that I should. I neither laid the foundation of repentance, nor of believing the gospel, taking it for granted that all to whom I preached were believers, and that many of them "needed no repentance."

(b.) From the year 1729 to 1734, laying a deeper foundation of repentance, I saw a little fruit. But it was only a little; and no wonder, for I did not preach faith in the blood of the covenant.

(c.) From 1734 to 1738, speaking more of faith in Christ, I saw more fruit of my preaching and visiting from house to house, than ever I had done before, though I know not if any of those who were outwardly reformed were inwardly and thoroughly converted to God.

(d.) From 1738 to this time, speaking continually of Jesus Christ, laying Him only for the foundation of the whole building, making him all in all, the first and the last;—preaching only on this plan, "The kingdom of God is at hand. Repent ye, and believe the gospel"—the "Word of God ran" as fire among the dry weeds. It was "glorified" more and more, with multitudes crying out, "What must we do to be saved?" and afterwards witnessing, "By grace we are saved through faith."

(e.) I considered deeply with myself what I ought to do, whether to declare the things I had seen or not. I consulted the most serious friends I had. They all agreed I ought to declare them. The work itself was of such a kind as ought not to be concealed. Indeed, the unusual circumstances now attending it made it impossible that it should.

(f.) This very difficulty occurred: "Will not my speaking of this be boasting? At least, will it not be accounted so?" They replied, "If you speak of it as your own work, it will be vanity and boasting all over. But if you ascribe it wholly to God, if you give him all the praise, it will not. And if, after this, some will account it so still, you must be content, and bear the burden."

(g.) I gave up and transcribed my papers for the press, only labouring as far as possible to "render unto God the things which are God's," to give him the praise of his own work.

2. But this very thing you improve into a fresh objection. If I ascribe anything to God it is *enthusiasm*. If I do not (or if I do) it is *vanity and boasting*, supposing I mention it at all. What then can I do to escape your censure? "Why, be silent. Say nothing at all." I cannot, I dare not. Were I thus to please men, I could not be the servant of Christ.

You do not appear to have the least idea or conception of what is in the heart of one whom it pleases Him that works all in all to employ in a work of this kind. He is in no way eager to be at all employed in it. He starts back, again and again, not only because he readily foresees what shame, care, sorrow, reproach, what loss of friends, and of all that the world accounts dear, will inevitably follow, but much more because he (in some measure) knows himself.

This chiefly it is which causes him to cry out (many times, in the bitterness of his soul, when no human eye sees him) "Oh, Lord, send by whom you will send, only send not me! What am I? A worm! A dead dog! A man unclean in heart and lips!" When he dares no longer deny or resist, when he is at last "thrust out into the harvest," he looks on the right hand and on the left. He takes every step with fear and trembling, and with the deepest sense (such as words cannot express) of "who is sufficient for these things?"

Every gift which he has received of God for the furtherance of his Word, whether of nature or grace, heightens this fear and increases his jealousy over himself knowing that so much the stricter must the inquiry be when he gives an account of his stewardship. He is most of all jealous over himself when the work of the Lord prospers in his hand. He is then amazed and confounded before God. Shame covers his face. Yet when he sees that he ought "to praise the Lord for his goodness, and to declare the wonders which he does for the children of men," he is in difficulty. He knows not which way to turn. He cannot speak. He dares not be silent. It may be for a time he "keeps his mouth with a bridle; he holds his peace even from good. But his heart is hot within him," and constrains him at length to declare what God has done.

And this he then does in all simplicity, with "great plainness of speech," desiring only to commend himself to Him who "searcheth the heart and trieth the reins" and (whether his words are the savour of life or of death to others) to have that witness in himself, "As of sincerity, as of God, in the sight of God, speak we in Christ." If any man counts this boasting, he cannot help it. It is enough that a higher Judge stands at the door.

3. But you may say, "Why do you talk of the success of the gospel in England, which was a Christian country before you were born?" Was it indeed? Is it so at this day? I would explain myself a little on this topic also.

And, (a.) none can deny that the people of England, in general, are called Christians. They are called so, a few only excepted, by others as well as by themselves. But I presume no man will say that the name makes the thing, that men are Christians simply because they are called so. (b.) It must be admitted that the people of England, generally speaking, have been christened or baptized. But neither can we infer, "These were once baptized. Therefore they are Christians now." (c.) It is admitted that many of those who were once baptized and are called Christians to this day hear the Word of God, attend public prayers, and partake of the Lord's Supper. But neither does this prove that they are Christians. Notwithstanding this, some of them live in open sin. Others (though not conscious to themselves of hypocrisy, yet) are utter strangers to the religion of the heart. They are full of pride, vanity, covetousness, ambition, of hatred, anger, malice, or envy; and consequently are no more scriptural Christians than the open drunkard or common swearer.

Now, these being removed, where are the Christians from whom we may properly term England a Christian country?—the men who have the mind which was in Christ, and who walk as he also walked? Where are those whose inmost soul is renewed after the image of God and who are outwardly holy as He who has called them is holy? There are doubtless a few such to be found. To deny this would be lack of candour. But how few! How thinly scattered up and down! As for a visible Christian Church, or a body of Christians visibly united together, where is this to be seen?

> *Ye different sects, who all declare,*
> *Lo! here is Christ, or, Christ is there!*
> *Your stronger proofs divinely give,*
> *And show me where the Christians live!*

What use is it, what good end does it serve, to term England a Christian country? (Although it is true, that most of the natives are called Christians, have been baptized, frequent the church services; and although a real Christian is here and there to be found, "as a light shining in a dark place.")

Does it do any honour to our great Master, among those who are not called by his name? Does it recommend Christianity to the Jews, the Mohammedans, or the avowed heathens? Surely no one can conceive it does. It only makes Christianity stink in their nostrils. Does it answer any good end with regard to those on whom this worthy name is called? I fear not, but rather an exceeding bad one. Does it not keep multitudes easy in their heathen practice? Does it not make or keep still greater numbers satisfied with their heathen tempers? Does it not directly tend to make both the one and the other imagine that they are what indeed they are not — that they are Christians — while they are utterly without Christ, and without God in the world?

To close this point: If men are not Christians till they are renewed after the image of Christ, and if the people of England in general are not thus renewed, why do we term them so? The god of this world has long blinded their hearts. Let us do nothing to increase that blindness, but rather labour to recover them from that strong delusion, that they may no longer believe a lie.

4. Let us labour to convince all mankind, that to be a real Christian is to love the Lord our God with all our heart, and to serve him with all our strength; to love our neighbour as ourselves, and therefore do every man as we would he should do us. Oh, no, you say, "Had you confined yourselves to these great points, there would have been no objection against your doctrine. But the doctrines you have distinguished yourselves by are not the love of God and man, but many false and pernicious errors." (Page 104.)

I have again and again, with all the plainness I could, declared what our constant doctrines are by which we are distinguished only from heathens, or nominal Christians not from any that worship God in spirit and in truth. Our main doctrines, which include all the rest, are three—that of repentance, of faith, and of holiness. The first of these we consider, as it were, the porch of religion; the next, the door; the third, religion itself.

That repentance or conviction of sin which is always previous to faith (either in a higher or lower degree, as it pleases God) we describe in words to this effect:

"When men feel in themselves the heavy burden of sin, see damnation to be the reward of it, see with the eye of their mind the horror of hell they tremble, they quake, and are inwardly touched with sorrowfulness of heart. They cannot but help accuse themselves and open their grief unto Almighty God, and call him for mercy. This being done seriously, their mind is so occupied—partly with sorrow and heaviness, partly with an earnest desire to be delivered from this danger of hell and damnation—that all desire for meat and drink is laid aside, and loathing of all worldly things and pleasure comes in place. So that nothing then pleases them more than to weep, to lament, to mourn, and both with words and behaviour of body to show themselves weary of life."

Now permit me to ask, What if, before you had observed that these were the very words of our own Church, one of your acquaintance or parishioners had come and told you that ever since he heard a sermon at the Foundery he "saw damnation" before him "and saw with the eye of his mind the horror of hell?" What if he had "trembled and quaked," and been so occupied "partly with sorrow and heaviness, partly with an earnest desire to be delivered from the danger of hell and damnation," as to "weep, to lament, to mourn, and both with words and behaviour to show himself weary of life?" Would you have hesitated to say, "Here is another 'deplorable instance' of the 'Methodists driving men to distraction!' See 'into what excessive terrors, frights, doubts, and perplexities, they throw weak and well-meaning men, quite oversetting their understandings and judgments and making them liable to all these miseries!'"

I dare not refrain from adding one plain question, which I plead with you to answer, not to me but to God: Have you ever experienced this repentance yourself? Did you ever "feel in yourself that heavy burden of sin," of sin in general, more especially, inward sin; of pride, anger, lust, vanity? Of (what is all sin in one) that carnal mind which is enmity, essential enmity, against God? Do you know by experience what it is to "see with the eye of the mind the horror of hell?" Was "your mind" ever so "occupied, partly with sorrow and heaviness, partly with an earnest desire to be delivered from this danger of hell and damnation, that even all desire for meat and drink" was taken away, and you "loathed all worldly things and pleasure?" Surely if you had known what it is to have the "arrows of the Almighty" thus "sticking fast in you," you could not so lightly have condemned those who now cry out, "The pains of hell come about me; the sorrows of death compass me, and the overflowings of ungodliness make me afraid."

5. Concerning the gate of religion—(if it may be allowed so to speak,) the true, Christian, saving faith—we believe it implies abundantly more

than an assent to the truth of the Bible. Even the devils believe that Christ was born of a virgin; that he performed all kind of miracles; that for our sakes he suffered a most painful death to redeem us from death everlasting. These articles of our faith the very devils believe, and so they believe all that is written in the Old and New Testament. Yet for all this faith, they are but devils. They remain still in their damnable estate, lacking the very true Christian faith.

"The right and true Christian faith is not only to believe that the Holy Scriptures and the articles of our faith are true, but also to have a sure trust and confidence to be saved from everlasting damnation through Christ." Perhaps it may be expressed more clearly thus: "A sure trust and confidence which a man has in God, that by the merits of Christ his sins are forgiven, and he is reconciled to the favour of God."

For giving this account of Christian faith (as well as the preceding account of repentance, both which I have here also purposely described in the very terms of the Homilies) I have been again and again, for nearly these eight years past, accused of enthusiasm, sometimes by those who spoke to my face,—either in conversation, or from the pulpit:—but more frequently by those who chose to speak in my absence, and not seldom from the press. I wait for those who judge this to be enthusiasm to bring forth their strong reasons. Till then I must continue to account all these the "words of truth and soberness."

6. Religion itself (I choose to use the very words with which I described it long ago) we define, "The loving God with all our heart, and our neighbour as ourselves; and in that love abstaining from all evil and doing all possible good to all men."

The same meaning we have sometimes expressed a little more at large thus: "Religion we conceive to be no other than love; the love of God and of all mankind; the loving God 'will all our heart, and soul, and strength,' as having 'first loved us,' as the fountain of all the good we have received, and of all we ever hope to enjoy; and the loving every soul which God has made, every man on earth, as our own soul.

"This love we believe to be the medicine of life, the never-failing remedy for all the evils of a disordered world, for all the miseries and vices of men. Wherever this is, there are virtue and happiness going hand in hand. There is humbleness of mind, gentleness, patience, the whole image of God, and at the same time, a peace that passes all understanding, and joy unspeakable and full of glory.

"This religion we long to see established in the world — a religion of love, and joy, and peace — having its seat in the heart, in the inmost soul, but ever showing itself by its fruits; continually springing forth, not only in all innocence (for love works no ill to his neighbour) but likewise in every kind of good deed, spreading virtue and happiness all around it."

If this can be proved by Scripture or reason to be enthusiastic or erroneous doctrine, we will then plead guilty to the indictment of "teaching error and enthusiasm." But if this is the genuine religion of Christ, then will all who advance this charge against us be found false witnesses before God in the day when he shall judge the earth.

7. However, with regard to the fruits of our teaching you say, "It is to be feared, the numbers of serious men who have been perplexed and deluded are much greater than the numbers of notorious sinners who have been brought to repentance and good life." (Page 113) "Indeed, if you could prove that the Methodists were, in general, very wicked people before they followed you, and that all you have been teaching them is the love of God and their neighbour, and a care to keep his commandments, which accordingly they have done since, you would stop the mouths of all adversaries at once. But we have great reason to believe that the generality of the Methodists, before they became so, were serious, regular, and well-disposed people." (Page 103.)

If the question were proposed—"Which are greater, the numbers of serious men who have been perplexed and deluded, or of notorious sinners who have been brought to repentance and good life," by these preachers throughout England, within seven years?—it might be difficult for you to locate the conclusion. For England is a place of wide dimensions, nor is it easy to make a satisfactory computation, unless you confine yourself within a smaller compass. Suppose then we were to contract the question in order to make it a little less unwieldy. We will bound our inquiry, for the present, within a square of three or four miles. It may be certainly known by candid men, both what has been and what is now done within this distance. From this point they may judge of those fruits elsewhere, which they cannot be so particularly informed of.

Inquire then, "Which are greater, the numbers of serious men, perplexed and deluded by these teachers, or of notorious sinners brought to repentance and good life," within the forest of Kingswood? Many indeed of the inhabitants are nearly as they were. They are not much better or worse for their preaching because the neighbouring Clergy and Gentry have successfully laboured to deter them from hearing it. But between three and four hundred of those who would not be deterred are now under the care of those preachers.

Now, what number of these were serious Christians before? Were fifty? Were twenty? Were ten? Perhaps there might five such be found, but it is a question whether there could or not. The remainder were great, open sinners, common swearers, drunkards, Sabbath-breakers, whoremongers, plunderers, robbers, implacable, unmerciful, wolves and bears in the shape of men. Do you desire instances of more "notorious sinners" than these? I know not if Turkey or Japan can afford them. And what do you include in "repentance and good life?" Give the strictest definition that you are able, and I will assert, these once notorious sinners shall be weighed in that balance, and not found lacking.

8. Not that all the Methodists (so called) "were very wicked people before they followed us." There are those among them, and not a few, who are able to stop the boasting of those that despise them, and to say, "Whereinsoever any of you is bold, I am bold also." Only they "count all these things but loss, for the excellency of the knowledge of Christ Jesus." But these we found, as it were, when we sought them not. We went forth to "seek that which was lost" (more eminently lost) "to call" the most flagrant, hardened, desperate "sinners to repentance." To this end we preached in the Horsefair at Bristol, in Kingswood, in Newcastle; among the colliers in Staffordshire, and the tinners in Cornwall; in Southwark, Wapping, Moorfields, Drury Lane, at London. Did any man ever pick out such places as these in order to find "serious, regular, well-disposed people?" How many such might then be in any of them I know not. But this I know, that four in five of those who are now with us were not of that number, but were "wallowing in their blood," till God by us said them, "Live."

Sir, I willingly put the whole cause on this issue: What are the general consequences of this preaching? Are there more weeds or wheat?—more "good men destroyed" (that is the proper question) or "wicked men saved?" The last place where we began constant preaching is a part of Wiltshire and Somersetshire, near Bath. Now, let any man inquire at Rhode, Bradford, Wrexall, or among the colliers at Coleford, (1.)

What kind of people were those "before they followed these men?" (2.) What are the main doctrines they have been teaching for this last year? (3.) What effect have these doctrines had upon their followers? What manner of lives do they lead now? If you do not find, (1.) That three in four of these were, two years ago, notoriously wicked men; (2.) That the main doctrines they have heard since were, "Love God and your neighbour, and carefully keep his commandments;" and (3.) That they have since exercised themselves in this, and continue so to do—I say if you, or any reasonable man who will be at the pains to inquire, does not find this to be an unquestionable fact, I will openly acknowledge myself an enthusiast, or whatsoever else you shall please to style me.

Only one caution I would give to such an inquirer. Let him not ask the colliers of Coleford, "Were not the generality of you, before you followed these men, serious, regular, well-disposed people?" Were you not "offended at the profaneness and debauchery of the age?" And "was it not this disposition which at first made you liable to receive these impressions?" (*Second Letter*, p. 103.) Because if he talks thus to some of those who do not yet "follow these men," perhaps he will not live to bring back their answer.

9. But will this, or a thousand such instances as this, "stop the mouths of all adversaries at once?" Oh, Sir, would one expect such a thought as this in one that had read the Bible? What if you could convert as many sinners as St. Paul himself? Would that "stop the mouths of all your adversaries?" Yes, if you could convert three thousand at one sermon, still you would be so far from "stopping all their mouths at once" that the greater part of them would gnash upon you with their teeth, and cry, "Away with such a fellow from the earth!"

I never, therefore, expect "to persuade the world," the majority of mankind, that I "have been" for some years "advancing nothing" but what has a clear, immediate connection with "the true knowledge and love of God." God has been pleased to use me, a weak, vile worm, in reforming many of my fellow-sinners and making them, at this day, living witnesses of "inward and pure religion." Many of these, "from living in all sin, are quite changed, are become" so far "holy, that" though they are not "free from all sin," yet no sin has dominion over them. And yet I do firmly believe, "it is nothing but downright prejudice, to deny or oppose any of these particulars." (*Preface*, page 5.)

"Allow Mr. Wesley," you say, "but these few points, and he will defend his conduct beyond exception." That is most true. If I have indeed "been advancing nothing but the true knowledge and love of God;" if God has made me an instrument in reforming many sinners, and bringing them to "inward and pure religion;" and if many of these continue holy to this day, and free from all willful sin, then may I, even I, use those awful words, "He that despiseth me, despiseth Him that sent me." But I never expect the world to allow me one of these points.

However, I must go on as God shall enable me. I must lay out whatsoever he intrusts me with (whether others will believe I do it or not) in advancing the true Christian knowledge of God, and the love and fear of God among men. I must go on reforming (if so be it please him to use me still) those who are yet without God in the world, and in propagating inward and pure religion—righteousness, peace, and joy in the Holy Ghost.

10. But you believe I only corrupt those who were good Christians before, teaching them to revile and censure their neighbours, and to abuse the Clergy, never mind all their meekness and gentleness, as I do myself. "I must declare," say you, "we have in general answered your pretence with all meekness and temper. The ranting and name-calling has been chiefly on the side of the Methodists." (*Second Letter*, page 16.)

Your first complaint ran thus: "How have such abuses as these been thrown out by you against our regular Clergy, not the highest or the worthiest excepted!" (*Remarks*, p. 15) I answered, "I am altogether clear in this matter, as often as it has been objected. Neither do I desire to receive any other treatment from the Clergy than they have received from me to this day." (Page 399)

You reply, (1.) "One instance of your misrepresenting and injuring a Preacher of our Church mentioned." (*Second Letter*, p. 105) *Mentioned!* Well, but did you *prove* it was an injury or misrepresentation? I know not that you once attempted it. (2.) You next quote part of a letter from the *Third Journal* (Vol. I. p. 184) where, according to your account, the "most considerable of our Clergy are abused, and at once accused in a very gross manner." (*Second Letter*, p. 106.) Set down the whole paragraph, and I will prove that this also is naked truth and not abuse at all. You say, (3.) "You approved of Whitefield's ranting against the Clergy."

I say, "Mr. Whitefield preached concerning the 'Holy Ghost, which all who believe are to receive,' not without a just, though severe, censure of those who preach as if there were no Holy Ghost." (Vol. I. p. 210.) Nor is this ranting, but melancholy truth. I have myself heard several preach in this manner. (4.) You cite my words: "Woe unto you, you blind leaders of the blind! How long will you pervert the right ways of the Lord?" and add, "I appeal to yourself, whether you did not design this reflection against the Clergy in general who differ from you." No more than I did against Moses and Aaron. I expressly specify whom I intend: "You who tell the mourners in Zion, Much religion has made you mad." You say, (5.) (with a N. B.,) "All the Clergy who differ from you, you style so (page 225) in which, and the foregoing page, you causelessly slander them as speaking of their own holiness as that for the sake of which, on account of which, we are justified before God."

Let any serious person read over those pages. I slander no man there. I speak what I know, what I have both heard and read. The men are alive, and the books are available. And the same conclusion I now defend, concerning that part of the Clergy who preach or write thus; *viz.,* if they preach the truth as it is in Jesus, I am found a false witness before God. But if I preach the way of God in truth, then they are blind leaders of the blind. (6.) You quote those words, "Nor can I be said to intrude into the labours of those who do not labour at all, but allow thousands of those for whom Christ died to perish for lack of knowledge." (Vol. I. p. 214.) I wrote that letter near Kingswood. I would to God the observation were not terribly true! (7.) The first passage you cite from the *Earnest Appeal* (pages 25, 26) evidently relates to a few only among the Clergy. If the charge is true of but one in five hundred, it abundantly supports my reasoning. (8.) In the next (*Ibid.* page 30) I address all those, and those only, who affirm that I preach for gain.

You conclude: "The reader has now before him the manner in which you have been pleased to treat the Clergy. Your late sermon is too fresh an instance of the like treatment of the Universities." (*Second Letter*, p. 107.) It is an instance of speaking the truth in love. So I desire all mankind may treat me. Nor could I have said less either to the University or the Clergy without sinning against God and my own soul.

11. But I must explain myself a little on that practice which you so often term "abusing the Clergy." I have many times great sorrow

and heaviness in my heart on account of these my brethren. This sometimes constrains me to speak to them in the only way which is now in my power, and sometimes, though rarely, to speak of them, of a few, not all in general. In either case, I take special care, (1.) To speak nothing but the truth. (2.) To speak this with all plainness; and (3) With love, and in the spirit of meekness. Now, if you will call this *abusing, ranting,* or *name-calling,* you must. But still I dare not refrain from it. I must thus rant, thus abuse sinners of all sorts and degrees, unless I will perish with them.

When I first read your declaration, that our brethren "in general had treated us with all meekness and temper," I had thoughts of spreading before you a few of the flowers which they have strewed upon us with no sparing hand. But on reflection, I judged it better to leave it alone. Let them die and be forgotten!

As to those of the people called *Methodists,* whom you suppose to "rant at and abuse the Clergy," and to "call names and censure their neighbours," I can only say, Which are they? Show me the men. If it appears, that any of those under my care habitually "call names" or "censure" others, whether Clergy or laity, I will make them an example for the benefit of all the rest.

Concerning you, I believe I was afraid without cause. I do not think you advanced a willful untruth. This was a rash word. I hereby openly retract it, and ask pardon of God and you.

To draw toward a conclusion: Whoever they are that "despise me, and make no account of my labours," I know that they are "not in vain in the Lord," and that I have not "fought as one that beateth the air." I still see (and I praise "the Father of Lights, from whom every good and perfect gift descendeth") a continual increase of pure religion and undefiled, of the love of God and man, of the "wisdom" which is "pure and peaceable, gentle, and easy to be entreated, full of mercy, and of good fruits." I see more and more of those "who before lived in a thorough contempt of God's ordinances, and of all duties, now zealously discharging their duties to God and man, and walking in all his ordinances blameless." A few indeed I have seen draw back to damnation, chiefly through a fear of being "too righteous." And here and there one has fallen into Calvinism, or turned aside to the Moravians. But, I doubt not, these "are in a better state" than they were before they heard us. I admit they are in error, oh, yes, and may die therein, yet who dares affirm they will perish everlastingly? But had they died in gross sin, we are sure they would have fallen into "the fire that never shall be quenched."

I have now considered, as far as my time would permit (not everything in your letter, whether of importance or not, but) those points which I conceived to be of the greatest weight. That God may lead us both into all truth, and that we may not drop our love in the pursuit of it, is the continual prayer of,

Reverend Sir,
Your friend and servant for Christ's sake,

JOHN WESLEY
June 17 , 1746

Endnotes

1. In Part 2, the Preface to the answer to Mr. Tucker, *The Principles of a Methodist.*
2. Vol. I. pp. 295, 296, of the present Edition.—Edition VIII.
3. Vol. I. pp. 163, 165, 176, 231, 264, 307, of the present Edition.—Edit. Vol. VIII.